how to Minister Among Older Adults

As Life's Journey Continues

Charles T. Knippel

CONCORDIA PUBLISHING HOUSE · SAINT LOUIS

This book is dedicated to the Rev. Elroy (Roy) Brockopp and teacher Duane Hingst who developed resources for ministry among older adults while serving as part-time co-managers of Older Adult Ministries of the Board for World Relief and Human Care Ministries of The Lutheran Church—Missouri Synod. Much of their invaluable work is incorporated into this book.

3558 S. Jefferson Ave., St. Louis, MO 63118-3968
1-800-325-3040 • www.cph.org

Manufactured in the United States of America

Library of Congress Cataloging-in-Publication Data

Knippel, Charles T., 1927-
How to minister among older adults : as life's journey continues / Charles T. Knippel.
p. cm.
ISBN 0-570-05305-6
1. Church work with older people--Lutheran Church--Missouri Synod. I. Title.
BV4435.K59 2005
259'.3—dc22 2005013588

1 2 3 4 5 6 7 8 9 10 14 13 12 11 10 09 08 07 06 05

How to Minister Among Older Adults

CONTENTS

Abbreviations

AC	Augsburg Confession
LW	Luther, Martin. *Luther's Works*. American Edition. General editors Jaroslav Pelikan and Helmut T. Lehmann. 56 vols. St. Louis: Concordia, and Philadelphia: Muhlenberg and Fortress, 1955–1986.
Tappert	Tappert, Theodore G. ed. *The Book of Concord*. Philadelphia: Fortress, 1959.

PREFACE

I AM PLEASED TO CONTINUE MY SERVICE in pastoral ministry during my retirement years by writing this book on how to minister among older adults. I have had opportunities to learn from others and reflect on my own experiences as a family member, a pastor, and an older adult.

I am grateful to Concordia Publishing House for the invitation to write this book in consultation with the Rev. Elroy (Roy) Brockopp and Mr. Duane Hingst. At the time of invitation, both of these men, even though they were retired from full-time professional church work, were serving as part-time co-managers of Older Adult Ministries of the Board for World Relief and Human Care Ministries of The Lutheran Church—Missouri Synod. The Rev. Brockopp served as a parish pastor for 17 years. Later, he served as executive director of the Council of Lutheran Churches in St. Louis and as vice-president of outreach ministries for the Lutheran Altenheim Society of St. Louis. Duane Hingst is a former parochial school teacher and principal and Missouri District Director of Lutheran Schools.

As co-managers of Older Adult Ministries, Roy Brockopp and Duane Hingst wrote extensively and presented workshops throughout The Lutheran Church—Missouri Synod to encourage congregations to enhance Christian ministry among older adults. This book makes use of much of their research and written materials, as well as my own reflections, inquiries, studies, and experiences related to older adult ministries. I am deeply indebted to Brockopp and Hingst for their contributions to this publication, and consider them to be co-authors.

With thanksgiving to God for the opportunity to write this book, I sincerely hope and pray that it will be helpful to the readers in intentionally shaping and facilitating ministry among older adults.

INTRODUCTION

THE URGENT NEED FOR THIS BOOK is underscored by the fact that the number of older adults in Christian congregations and their communities is increasing rapidly and will continue to increase even more so in the years to come. We have done too little and need to do much more in the area of service among older adults.

In this book I speak of how to serve *among* older adults rather than focusing only on ministry *to* or *by* older adults. I view the concept of ministry *among* older adults to include ministry both *to* and *by* older adults and most certainly ministry *with* them. The word *among* indicates that all of us who are concerned with older adult ministries serve in the midst of older adults. We minister both to be of service to them and to encourage them to use their gifts to minister, together with us, to others, including other older adults.

Just as the word *among* is important in this book, so is the word *intentional*. The word *intentional* implies that we are not simply to hope that ministry among older adults will happen as we go about traditional tasks of the Christian congregation. *Intentional* means that we must thoughtfully and carefully plan and carry out ministry among older adults.

In this book I invite you, the reader, to think with me not only about retired older adults but also those who are nearing retirement. I also wish to lead you to consider intergenerational relationships in the Christian congregation for the purpose of facilitating the ministry of younger persons to the older, the older to the younger, and the younger and older together.

The love of God the Father in His Son Jesus both motivates and equips us for Christian service, enabling us to do ministry among older adults.

As we go about our task, our journey will take us to the Bible for counsel and for the means to accomplish our goals. Our journey will take us to Christ crucified and risen from the dead. We will remember again and again that He paid for our sins by suffering the condemnation we deserve, and that by His suffering and death on the cross we have forgiveness of sins before the Father through faith in Him. We remember that with the gift of the forgiveness of sins God places us in His family and renews us for Christian living and serving. The love of God the Father in His Son Jesus both motivates and equips us for Christian service, enabling us to do ministry among older adults.

We will find it helpful to confer with those who have lived before us and have wisdom to share with us about older adults. I have especially valued the opportunity to review biblical insights provided by Dr. Martin Luther. I hope that you will find his Bible-based instruction concerning the doctrine of the Christian's calling, or vocation, especially helpful in the consideration of older adult living.

This is very much a "how to" book. I have included specific ideas and suggestions for serving among older adults. Everyone interested in ministry among older adults will find something here to try, to adapt, to implement, and the encouragement to plan additional actions and activities.

What I write is primarily for pastors, other church professionals, and leaders of Christian congregations to use in facilitating ministry among older adults. However, this book has meaning for all congregation members, both young and old, who want to serve others of all ages in an effective manner, who desire to help all members of the congregation serve one another and those still outside the Christian fellowship.

Before we consider the chapters to come, I wish to make clear that when I speak of ministry or ministering among older adults, I am *not* using the words *ministry* or *ministering* to refer to the pastoral office, the God-instituted Office of the Holy Ministry of Word and Sacraments, even though pastors carry out their unique ministry also among older adults. Those called to the Office of the Holy Ministry of Word and Sacraments are public ministers, that is, they are set aside by God to serve on behalf of a Christian congregation and for the benefit of God's people. They do this by proclaiming and applying the Word of God and by administering the Sacraments of Holy Baptism and the Lord's Supper.

When I write about ministry among older adults in this book, I am referring to the service of all Christians, not exclusively the service of the called and ordained ministers of the Church or other church professionals. These called and ordained or commissioned ministers of the Church are God's good and necessary gifts to the Church. Their vocations are vitally important for shaping the ministry (the Christian service or serving) of all God's people, but this book does not focus on their ministries, even though it seeks to offer assistance to them, as well as to all leaders and members of Christian congregations.

I am grateful to be able to share with you discoveries that have enriched my life that I hope will enrich your life and your ministry among older adults. May the Father's blessing rest upon this work for the sake of His Son, Jesus.

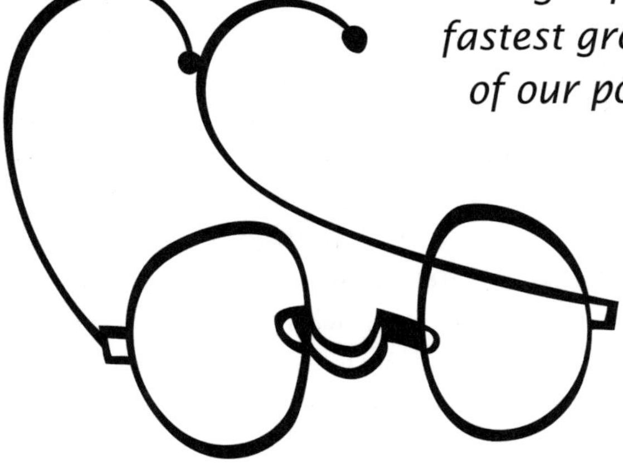

Americans over the age of 65 are the fastest growing part of our population.

1 Older Adults in the Present and Future

Increasing Numbers

At the beginning of the twenty-first century, life's journey continues for a longer time for a larger number of people. The increasing number of older adults in the United States makes this book important for the Church. We need to earnestly be concerned about ministry among the growing number of older adults who are living longer than ever before.

In recent years much has been said and written about the coming "age wave." Data provided by the 2000 United States Census Bureau support the belief that a large wave of older adults is here and is intensifying year after year.[1] This 2000 and other United States census data and pertinent information provided by the Administration on Aging are the sources for most of the statistics incorporated into this chapter.

In the United States we typically think of older adults as persons, usually retired, who are at least 65 years of age. For example, the Census 2000 Brief, "The 65 Years and Over Population: 2000" defines the older population as people 65 years and over.[2] To a large extent our discussion employs this same understanding because a great deal of the available data considers older adults in this manner. However, much of what we discuss will relate to retired persons, and those preparing to retire, who are younger than 65. Many retire from their full-time life's work at 65, 62, and even younger.[3] However, for some, the retirement age is gradually changing upward. In 2004 only those retiring at age 65 and 10 months could receive unreduced Social Security benefits. A person could still retire at age 62, but with full benefits reduced by 24.2 percent. Those retiring between 2005 and 2016 will be able to receive unreduced benefits only at age 66. For those retiring at 62 there will be a 25 percent reduction in benefits.[4]

The 2000 U.S. census counted 35 million people 65 years of age and over. This indicated an increase in this age group of 12 percent since 1990.[5] Strange to say, this percentage showed that the number of people over 65 in the year 2000 did not grow faster than the total population for the first time in United States history.[6] However, this does not mean that the number of persons 65 and over is decreasing. It only reflects a relatively low number of births in the late 1920s and early 1930s. This trend will reverse radically in the future, especially as the 77 million Boomers born from 1946 through 1964 begin reaching age 65 in 2011.[7]

Although the percentage increase of people 65 years and over was less than in years past, the number of persons in this age group, as we have noted, totals a formidable 35 million. Since 1900, the percentage of Americans 65 years of age and over has more than tripled, and the number has increased 11 times.[8] Americans over the age of 65 are the fastest growing part of our population. In fact, the population over the age of 65 is increasing twice as fast as the population as a whole. Of interest, the number of persons over the age of 100 has doubled in the last 10 years.[9]

The older population is itself getting older. Life expectancy has climbed to 76.9 years.[10] In 2000 the 65 to 74 age group (18.4 million) was eight times larger than in 1900. The 75 to 84 age group (12.4 million) was 16 times larger, and the 85 and over group (4.2 million) was 34 times larger.[11] During the 1990s the most rapid growth of the older population occurred in the oldest age groups. People are living longer. The population 85 years and over increased by 38 percent, from 3.1 million to 4.2 million. People 75 to 84 years old increased by 23 percent.[12]

The projections for the number of persons 65 years and older are staggering. The older population will mushroom between 2011 and 2030, when the Baby Boomers, born between 1946 and 1964, will reach 65. Projections indicate the number of persons 65 and over will be 70 million in 2030, 20 percent of the population and more than twice their number in 2000.[13]

The "age wave" is upon us. There is no doubt that the number of older adults is rapidly increasing, and that older people are living longer. As noted, today's life expectancy is 76 plus years. A man 65 years old can expect to live another 16.3 years, and a 65-year-old woman another 19.2 years. A man 85 years old can expect to live another 5.6 years, and an 85-year-old woman another 6.7 years.[14]

Estimates indicate that between 16 and 18 percent of The Lutheran Church—Missouri Synod members are over 65. Some congregations report that more than 30 percent of their members are well into their 60s.[15] These numbers and population projections mandate Christian congregations to give serious attention to ministry among older adults. Increasing attention to the growing number of older adults is taking place in the arenas of education, business, and science. The Church that, for so long, has focused its attention primarily on younger people, cannot do less. Indeed, the Church must be engaged earnestly and expansively in ministry among older adults.

A Profile of Older Adults

In 2000 women outnumbered men in the 65 and over age group. There were 14.4 million men and 20.6 million women.[16] In 2001 there were over four times as many widows (8.49 million) as widowers (2.0 million). The male-female ratio drops steadily with age.[17]

The median income for older adults in 2002 was $19,686 for males and $11,313 for females. From 2000 to 2002 the median income decreased by 2.6 percent for older people. According to the Social Security Administration, Social Security was the major source of income for 90 percent of older people.[18] About 3.4 million older persons lived below the poverty level in 2001. Another 2.2 million older adults were classified as "near poor."[19]

We are inclined to think that most older adults live in nursing homes. However, a relatively small number lived in nursing homes in 2000. While the percentage increases with age, only 4.5 percent of the older population lived in nursing homes. Over half (55 percent) of non-institutionalized persons lived with their spouse in 2000. About 30 percent lived alone.[20] In 1997 approximately 633,000 grandparents aged 65 or over maintained their own households in which grandchildren were present. In addition, 510,000 grandparents over 65 lived in homes in which their grandchildren were present.[21]

Individual Needs

We may have found our review of statistics to be somewhat tedious. But consideration of relevant statistics is valuable because such a survey tells us much about the necessity of ministry among older adults and points to some of their pressing needs. Like every age group, older adults have needs identified distinctly with their set. What their specific needs are depends on many factors. Needs are not identical for each older adult.

Many older adults are independent, healthy, and happy about their lifestyles. They have a wholesome sense of worth and energetically live each day in ways that satisfy themselves and benefit others. They have no pressing health issues or income concerns. As a group, today's older adults are healthier, more active, and better educated than they have ever been.

However, the information we have examined indicates that many older adults do have financial and health concerns and needs. A significant number of older adults are trying to adjust to life without their spouse. They continue on a day-by-day basis to deal with the grief they experience as the result of a spouse's death and many attendant losses. They frequently grieve about the loss of youthful health and strength, the family home, accustomed daily living patterns, emotional support, and income. They suffer from loneliness, depression, boredom, fear of living alone, and fear of dying. Many have increasing concerns about their value, strength, health, and how to afford necessary medical care and medicines. Some are not sure about their ability to carry out family responsibilities, such as caring for a grandchild or other dependent relatives. Sometimes they suffer from neglect and abuse by family members or those who care for them. Those who live in nursing homes likely feel even more alienated from their previous ways of living.

The Church's Present-Day Ministry

We need to ask ourselves whether the Church is adequately ministering among older adults. Some observers say that we are not ministering as effectively as God expects from His Church. Life in the Church today, they suggest, demonstrates that we have not focused sufficiently on ministry among older adults, and that we have neglected to cultivate both intergenerational ministry and the corresponding relationships that develop from it. Again, by *intergenerational ministry* I mean service by the younger to the older, service by the older to the younger, and service by both the younger and older, not only to each other, but to others and causes outside themselves.

God is the creator of human beings of all ages and in Jesus, His Son, has made available eternal salvation for both young and old.

2 The Christian View of Older Adults

All Loved By God

In some societies older adults are highly revered, and people have great love for them. In other societies older adults are looked down upon as useless human beings and are unloved by the people around them.

The Bible affirms that God loves all people of the world and therefore loves all older adults. St. John wrote, "For God so loved the world, that He gave His only Son, that whoever believes in Him should not perish but have eternal life" (John 3:16). To Titus, St. Paul wrote, "For the grace of God has appeared, bringing salvation for all people" (Titus 2:11).

God is the creator of human beings of all ages and in Jesus, His Son, has made available eternal salvation for both young and old. As the One who preserves all of His creation, God, in His love for people, gives good gifts to all and certainly also to all older adults, even those who are not yet in a saving relationship with Him. According to the Bible, God "makes His sun rise on the evil and on the good, and sends rain on the just and on the unjust" (Matthew 5:45). God preserves both "man and beast" (Psalm 36:6). The psalmist writes that God opens His hand and satisfies the desires of every living thing (Psalm 145:16).

Among His good gifts, God gives people an innate knowledge of Him (the natural knowledge of God) and knowledge of good and evil generated by the Law of God written in human hearts. These gifts are limited and often distorted by people. Nevertheless, God gives them the ability to use God-given knowledge that is rightly understood for their own physical and social welfare and that of others. This goodness of God flows from the ways He rules in the secular (temporal) realm with His left hand. This is in contrast with the ways He rules with His right hand in the spiritual realm through His saving revelation of Jesus Christ to provide people with spiritual and eternal benefits—forgiveness of sin, life, and salvation.

Esteemed by Scripture

The Bible holds older people in high esteem. The Sacred Scriptures show how God Himself regards older adults and how He wants us to value them. The Bible demonstrates how God used older persons to carry forward His divine plans. As called by God, Abraham left Haran to go to Canaan, when he had lived 75 of his 175 years. By God's will, Abraham became the father of his promised son Isaac when he was 100 years old. Moses had lived 80 of his 120 years when God used him to command Pharaoh to set His people free from their slavery in Egypt. By the design of God, David was still king of Israel when he died in his 71st year.

In the New Testament God gives special attention to a number of older people as He unfolds His plan of salvation in Jesus. He gave the priest Zechariah and his wife, Elizabeth, the blessing of being the parents of John the Baptizer, the forerunner and herald of Jesus. Luke says that "both were advanced in years" (Luke 1:7). After the birth of Jesus, at the time of His presentation in the temple, God allowed Simeon, who evidently was advanced in age, to hold the Lord's Christ, praise God, and speak of the Child's future (Luke 2:25–35). At the same time Anna, a prophetess, came upon the child Jesus. She gave thanks to God for Him and spoke "of Him to all who were waiting for the redemption of

Jerusalem" (Luke 2:36–38). Luke says of Anna that "she was advanced in years" (Luke 2:36). She was over 80 years of age.

In the Old Testament we find words in praise of old age. Psalm 92 says,

> The righteous flourish like the palm tree
> and grow like a cedar in Lebanon.
> They are planted in the house of the Lord;
> they flourish in the courts of our God.
> They still bear fruit in old age;
> they are ever full of sap and green,
> to declare that the Lord is upright;
> He is my rock, and there is no unrighteousness in Him.
> (Psalm 92:12–15)

In the book of Isaiah we hear God declare,

> Listen to me, O house of Jacob,
> all the remnant of the house of Israel,
> who have been borne by me from before your birth,
> carried from the womb;
> even to your old age I am He,
> and to gray hairs I will carry you.
> I have made, and I will bear;
> I will carry and will save. (Isaiah 46:3–4)

In his letter to Titus, St. Paul showed his concern for older Christians and declared their value and importance to others. He wrote,

> But as for you, teach what accords with sound doctrine. Older men are to be sober-minded, dignified, self-controlled, sound in faith, in love, and in steadfastness. Older women likewise are to be reverent in behavior, not slanderers or slaves to much wine. They are to teach what is good, and so train the young women to love their husbands and children, to be self-controlled, pure, working at home, kind, and submissive to their own husbands, that the word of God may not be reviled. (Titus 2:1–5)

St. Paul also wrote advice to Timothy about older men and women by which he demonstrated his great respect for them. "Do not rebuke an older man but encourage him as you would a father. Treat younger men like brothers, older women like mothers, younger women like sisters, in all purity" (1 Timothy 5:1–2). After these words, Paul gave instructions concerning the care of widows in the Christian congregation (1 Timothy 5:3–10).

Older people are valued by God, and are to be valued by God's people.

In his letter to Philemon, St. Paul spoke of himself as "an old man" (Philemon 9). Paul was old and in prison when he wrote to Philemon, but he was still very much an essential and effective minister of Jesus Christ even as "an old man." There was no man who could take his place in the ministry of the early church.

God, through the Bible, instructs us to hold older people in high esteem. Older people are valued by God, and are to be valued by God's people. Older people have significant contributions to make to the lives of both young and old.

Restored and Renewed

Like every Christian, older adult Christians are people restored and renewed by God. They are restored from their alienation from God to a right relationship with Him. They are renewed by the Holy Spirit to turn from a life controlled by disobedience to God toward Christian living and serving.

Christian older adults, like all Christians, are of great value before God because He has purchased and won them from sin, its condemnation and power, at a great price. Like all of us, they have been purchased and won by the innocent suffering and death of God's Son, who became a man and lived among us, until, after His resurrection from the dead, He ascended into heaven. In His suffering and dying on a cross, God's Son, Jesus, was their substitute before God and made good for their sinfulness and sin. He suffered the punishment due them for their sin. Through God's gift of faith in Jesus, God forgives their sins, makes them His own, and renews their lives. They are no longer slaves to sin and its destructive power, but they are highly treasured and cherished children of God, who has freed them from sin to live in His service.

The apostle Paul clearly teaches what we have summarized. "For our sake [God] made [Jesus] to be sin who knew no sin, so that in Him we might become the righteousness of God" (2 Corinthians 5:21). "[I]n Christ God was reconciling the world to Himself, not counting their trespasses against them" (2 Corinthians 5:19). "But when the fullness of time had come, God sent forth His Son, born of woman, born under the law, to redeem those who were under the law, so that we might receive adoption as sons" (Galatians 4:4–5). "For by grace you have been saved through faith. And this is not your own doing; it is the gift of God, not a result of works, so that no one may boast" (Ephesians 2:8–9). Then St. Paul goes on to say, "For we are His workmanship, created in Christ Jesus for good works, which God prepared beforehand, that we should walk in them" (Ephesians 2:10). St. Paul emphasizes that "if anyone is in Christ, he is a new creation. The old has passed away; behold, the new has come" (2 Corinthians 5:17). To be sure, none of us is perfect, because remnants of sin still live in us. But by the power of the Holy Spirit we strive to will and do what pleases God and benefits us and others.

Two Lutheran confessional documents speak biblically and eloquently about how it is that we, both young and old, are God's treasured people, forgiven and renewed. The basic Lutheran confession, the Augsburg Confession, states,

> It is also taught among us that we cannot obtain forgiveness of sin and righteousness before God by our own merits, works, or satisfactions, but that we receive forgiveness of sin and become righteous before God by grace, for Christ's sake, through faith, when we believe that Christ suffered for us and that for his sake our sin is forgiven and righteousness and eternal life are given to us. For God will regard and reckon this faith as righteousness, as Paul says in Romans 3:21–26 and 4:5.[1]

In his Small Catechism, Dr. Martin Luther speaks of Jesus Christ as the One

> who has redeemed me, a lost and condemned creature, delivered me and freed me from all sins, from death, and from the

power of the devil, not with silver and gold but with his holy and precious blood and with his innocent sufferings and death, in order that I may be his, live under him in his kingdom, and serve him in everlasting righteousness, innocence, and blessedness, even as he is risen from the dead and lives and reigns to all eternity.[2]

Christian older adults are a special people—people restored to God and renewed for godly living and serving.

In summary, we joyfully acknowledge that, through His gift to us of faith in Jesus as our Savior, God does great things in our lives. He enables us to trust in Jesus for the forgiveness of sins by which we become God's own people. Then, when God forgives our sins for Jesus' sake, He renews us to strive to live as His own. This is true of all believers in Jesus, both young and old. Christian older adults are a special people—people restored to God and renewed for godly living and serving. The process of becoming older does not change this in any way. It only brings people closer to the fullness of joy prepared by God for them in heaven.

A Letter from Luther

One particular writing of Martin Luther eloquently expresses his understanding of the value and importance of older adults as taught in Holy Scripture. This is a letter that Luther wrote to his aging and ailing father, Hans, in 1530. In this letter, which many consider to be one of Luther's finest writings, Luther shows his high regard for his father and teaches us how to look upon our parents and other older adults. Here I quote the opening paragraph of Luther's letter.

To my dear Father, Hans Luther, a citizen at Mansfeld in the valley:

Grace and peace in Christ Jesus, our Lord and Saviour. Amen.

Dear Father: James, my brother, has written me that you are seriously ill. As the weather is now bad, and as there is danger everywhere, and because of the season, I am worried about you. For even though God has thus far given to and preserved for you a strong, tough body, yet your age gives me anxious thoughts at this time—although regardless of this [worry], none of us is, or should be, sure of his life at any time. Therefore because of these circumstances I would have liked to come to you personally, but my good friends advised me against it, and have talked me out of it. I myself have to agree, for I did not dare to venture into danger at the risk of tempting God, since you know how lords and peasants feel toward me. It would be great joy for me, however, if it were possible for you and mother to be brought here to us; this my Katie, too, desires with tears, and we all [join her in this]. I hope we would be able to take care of you in the best way. Therefore I am sending Cyriac to see whether your weakness [will allow you to be moved]. For if according to God's will your illness turns out to be one either to life or to death, it would be a heartfelt joy for me (as would be only right) to be around you in person and to show, with filial faithfulness and service, my gratitude to God and to you, according to the Fourth Commandment.[3]

Challenge for the Church

God has much to say about older adults. What God teaches in the Bible about older adults challenges all of us who compose the membership of today's church to minister carefully and caringly among older adults. We are to minister to them and make it possible for them to use their faith, experiences, abilities, and skills to minister to others.

This challenge that confronts Christian congregations becomes much more essential as the number of older adults among us increases year by year. If, as is apparently true in many congregations, we are neglecting to carry forward purposeful and comprehensive ministry among older adults, we need to rise to the challenge that is before us.

3 Older Adults and Retirement Years

The Gift of Retirement

Today, retirement years are an experience that many people in past years did not enjoy. Most Americans now at age 65 have as much as one-third of their lives to live.[1] This has not always been the case. In 1900 life expectancy was 49.2 years. In 2000 it was 76.9 years.[2]

As we reflect on how life's journey has changed for many of us today, we realize the debt of gratitude we owe to our forefathers who have made it possible for us, by their lives and sacrifices, to enjoy the possibilities of longer life than they had and retirement opportunities they did not possess. Following in their steps, we have the privilege in our day to enrich the lives of others. There are multitudes of people in the modern third world and in many areas of the urban United States who do not enjoy the gifts that God has made available to many of us who read this book. For many, daily life is similar to that of the central figure in Upton Sinclair's book *The Jungle*. Jurgis Rudkos, a Lithuanian immigrant, came to the

United States with members of his family around the turn of the twentieth century to make his fortune. They came fortified with courage and hope. However, compelled to work in the dismal stockyards of a large city, they were cheated, abused, and oppressed on every side. They suffered privations of every sort. One by one the members of the unfortunate household died, but they worked to the last to do their part in the great struggle for a better life. This story illustrates how important it is for us who have richly blessed lives to do our part, as have our forefathers, in the great task of providing a better life for the underprivileged, both near to us and far from us.

This is most certainly true: Since 1900 life has significantly changed, and opportunities have expanded for many in these United States. In 1900 only 3 million Americans were 65 and older. Then came the year 2000, and the number grew to 35 million. Projections indicate that the number will be 40 million in 2010, 54 million in 2020, and 71 million in 2030. The projection for 2040 is 80 million.[3]

In reality, the number of people entering their retirement years in our day is notably larger than that of people reaching age 65. More and more people are retiring from their full-time occupations and professions earlier than age 65. As we have observed, today people are retiring at 50, 55, 60, and even earlier. Clearly, more and more people are reaching retirement age and will have longer years of retirement.[4]

Today much is being written especially about the coming wave of older adults who are Christians. Many suggest older adults are the future of the Church, and their vast numbers, rather than a younger population, will shape the Church of the first half of this twenty-first century. These are, and will be, exceptional people because most of these older adults will enjoy many healthy and highly productive years. They promise to become the most effective force of volunteers in history and outstanding witnesses to the Gospel of Jesus Christ.

What we have said about older adult Christians who retire may not apply to all retiring older adults, either professing Christians or non-Christians. This may be true especially of some Baby Boomers who will turn 65 in 2011. Much is written about the 77 million people who were born between 1946 and 1964. There are observers who say that many are "self-centered, self-seeking, self-interested, self-absorbed, self-indulgent and self-aggrandizing."[5]

For all retiring persons who fit this description in some ways and to some degree, God has words of counsel. Here are the words of Jesus: "For what does it profit a man to gain the whole world and forfeit his life? For what can a man give in return for his life?" (Mark 8:36–37). This passage and other biblical words of wisdom call all of us who are self-centered to repentance. Jesus calls us to be sorry for our sins of selfishness and to trust in Him for forgiveness for all narcissistic attitudes and actions. He richly forgives all who turn to Him as their Savior from sin and gives new direction and strength to serve others unselfishly.

> **vocation** *does not mean a job, occupation, or profession. Rather, the word vocation refers to a person's calling from God to serve in the place in life where God is pleased to have that service*

The bottom line is this: Retirement years are gifts of God to retirees. Graciously, God has made it possible for us to live longer. He has provided scientific and medical discoveries and innovations that generate and support longer life. Just as God has given longer life as a gift to us as individuals, so He has given our longer lives as a gift to society within and outside the Church. He has given us the opportunity to serve one another in love for the improvement of the quality of life, and especially for the expansion of the Christian mission for the salvation of people at home and abroad. The Lord of the Church, who directed His people to be "the light of the world" (Matthew 5:14), has multiplied our number and our length of time to let our "light to shine before others" so they praise God (Matthew 5:14–16). We live in days remarkably blessed by our generous and gracious God.

Truths about Christian Callings

No matter what our age, the days before retirement and early in retirement are times for us to consider and intentionally apply the Christian concept of *vocation* or *calling*. This is a concept that has its own unique meaning. Here vocation does not mean a job, occupation, or profession.

Rather, the word *vocation* refers to a person's calling from God to serve in the place in life where God is pleased to have that service.

The concept of the Christian vocation or calling, as we shall discover later in more detail, has an important bearing on our discussion of the retirement years of older adults and ministry among older adults. It provides the backdrop for us to consider how retired persons receive exciting and challenging opportunities from God that reshape their Christian lives according to His plan.

The clarification of the biblical concept of the Christian calling was an outstanding contribution of Martin Luther during the sixteenth century reformation of the church. He shaped a new understanding of the Christian calling through the energetic and ardent study of the Bible. He did this with a sense of urgency because of the unbiblical way the church of his day understood the concept of Christian calling. For example, the church of Luther's day taught that only a priest, nun, or monk had a Christian calling. The calling to be a monk and live the monastic life was considered more pleasing to God than other ways of Christian living. Moreover, this calling was looked upon as one that actually merited God's love and forgiveness. Luther had this to say about the teaching of the day:

> Furthermore, they [the pope, together with his priests and monks] have belittled Baptism and Christian vocations. Therefore it was necessary to enter special higher callings and orders, and to create a more exalted Baptism for the monks. In brief, they have introduced a special, self-devised sanctity, apart from and contrary to the common Word and order of God and the ordinary godly vocations. In this way alone they aspired to get to heaven or at least to assist others in attaining that goal. These things, they claim, gleam like precious gems. The others—plain Baptism, the Sacrament, father, mother, government, pious masters and mistresses in the home, servants and maids—they treat with scorn and regard as nothing.[6]

As Martin Luther studied the Scripture, he discovered that the concept of *call* or *calling* includes several biblical senses of meaning. First, the concept of calling means that God calls us by the Gospel to know and believe that Jesus is our Savior from sin, death, and hell. Luther stated this understanding in his explanation of the third article of the Apostles' Creed in the Small Catechism. There he wrote:

> I believe that by my own reason or strength I cannot believe in Jesus Christ, my Lord, or come to him. But the Holy Spirit has called me through the Gospel, enlightened me with his gifts, and sanctified and preserved me in true faith, just as he calls, gathers, enlightens, and sanctifies the whole Christian church on earth and preserves it in union with Jesus Christ in the one true faith.[7]

Luther expounded his thoughts in his Large Catechism, explaining:

> Neither you nor I could ever know anything of Christ, or believe in him and take him as our Lord, unless these were first offered to us and bestowed on our hearts through the preaching of the Gospel by the Holy Spirit. The work is finished and completed, Christ has acquired and won the treasure for us by his sufferings, death, and resurrection, etc. But if the work remained hidden and no one knew of it, it would have been all in vain, all lost. In order that this treasure might not be buried but put to use and enjoyed, God has caused the Word to be published and proclaimed, in which he has given the Holy Spirit to offer and apply to us this treasure of salvation.[8]

In his catechisms Luther faithfully expressed what the Bible teaches. God calls people to Himself by the Gospel, giving them saving faith in Jesus Christ for the forgiveness of sins. To the Christians in Thessalonica St. Paul wrote: "But we ought always to give thanks to God for you, brothers beloved by the Lord, because God chose you as the firstfruits to be saved, through sanctification by the Spirit and belief in the truth. To this He called you through our gospel, so that you may obtain the glory of our Lord Jesus Christ" (2 Thessalonians 2:13–14). He also proclaimed, "And those whom [God] predestined He also called, and those whom He called He also justified, and those whom He justified He also glorified" (Romans 8:30).

God, who calls people to Himself, does even more for His forgiven people. He renews His forgiven people by His Holy Spirit to serve Him and others as they live in the Church, the fellowship of His people. This truth is expressed by these words of St. Paul to the Ephesians:

> For by grace you have been saved through faith. And this is not your own doing; it is the gift of God, not a result of works, so that no one may boast. *For we are His workmanship, created in Christ Jesus for good works, which God prepared beforehand, that we should walk in them.* (Ephesians 2:8–10, *my emphasis*)

Also to the Ephesians the apostle Paul wrote:

> I therefore, a prisoner for the Lord, urge you to *walk in a manner worthy of the calling [to be a Christian] to which you have been called*, with all humility and gentleness, with patience, bearing with one another in love, eager to maintain the unity of the Spirit in the bond of peace. There is one body and one Spirit—just as you were called to the one hope that belongs to your call—one Lord, one faith, one baptism, one God and Father of all, who is over all and through all and in all. (Ephesians 4:1–6, *my emphasis*)

God leaves us without doubt. He calls us to a right relationship with Himself and to a new and eternal life of love and service empowered and guided by the Holy Spirit. God bids us to serve Him in our calling to be a Christian.

Second, this basic calling to be a Christian and to live the Christian life includes certain specific and individualized callings or vocations. This means that every Christian who has the calling to faith in Jesus and to live the life of love and service has multiple callings in life that are designed and approved by God's Law. In these individual callings we are to live out our calling to the Christian life. In these callings Christians live with love for others and in their service to the praise of God.

According to Luther, then, each one of us who is called by God to be believers in Christ has the calling to Christian living that is made up of various callings or vocations. These various callings are in one or more of the three orders of life—in the home, state, or church. Luther sometimes referred to these multiple callings as stations in life, and also spoke of callings as vocations. Among them are the vocations of father, mother, son, daughter, husband, wife, teacher, student, farmer, laborer, pastor, physician, scientist, engineer, secretary, lawyer, judge, or government worker. Most frequently, it seems that when Luther spoke of the calling of a person called to be a Christian, he was referring to a person's occupation, profession, or role of primary responsibility, such as the mother of a household who tends her baby. However, for Luther, one person who has the calling to be a farmer also has other callings, such as to be a husband, father, and citizen. A person who has the calling to be a student also has callings to be a son or daughter.

St. Paul affirmed that each and every Christian has a place in life assigned by the Lord and to which the Lord has called the Christian. He explained, "Only let each person lead the life that the Lord has assigned to him, and to which God has called him. This is my rule in all the churches" (1 Corinthians 7:17). As an example of the kinds of places in life to which he referred, Paul spoke of persons being a slave or being a freeman. He commented, "Were you a slave when called? Do not be concerned about it. But if you can gain your freedom, avail yourself of the opportunity. For he who was called in the Lord as a slave is a freedman of the Lord. Likewise he who was free when called is a slave of Christ" (1 Corinthians 7:21–22).

Martin Luther taught that each and every Christian called by God to faith has a primary calling, station, or responsibility in life. He wrote, "Thus every person surely has a calling. While attending to it he serves God. A king serves God when he is at pains to look after and govern his people. So do the mother of the household when she tends her baby, the father of a household when he gains a livelihood by working, and a pupil when he applies himself diligently to his studies."[9]

Martin Luther felt strongly that no calling is better than others before God or more pleasing to Him than others. He remarked, "Nor can anything so insignificant be done in a calling ordained by God that it is not pleasing to God. And if it is done in faith and in the Word, it excels all the miracles of all the popes and monks."[10] Luther observed that "the real chief points of godliness and of true religion are these: faith toward God, through which we receive remission of sins; invocation; thanksgiving; and confession; next, the works of our calling with reference to our neighbor, that you rule, prescribe, teach, comfort, exhort, make a living by working, etc."[11] He also declared, "Those who are in a lower class should know that their calling carries with it the same honor and lofty spirit that their masters or other, higher classes have; for whatever prestige or distinction attaches to their superiors, this the servants have in common with them, and the servants share in the honor for which they praise their masters."[12]

His reading of the Bible showed Luther that God Himself assigns Christians to their callings. "Shall I become impatient," said Luther, "or refuse to follow my calling? No. I shall rather reflect that God has manifold graces or forms of activity and allots them in accordance with His will. But it is our duty to obey God when He calls (Rom. 12:6; 1 Peter 4:10)."[13]

God always calls wisely and, when He makes His assignments, He certainly takes into consideration the gender, age, gifts, and abilities of the Christian. St. Paul highlights the goodness of God in bestowing gifts for the common good and stresses that each and every Christian is a member of the body of Christ with his or her own particular function (1 Corinthians 12). Luther, in discussing Christian calling, was referring to Paul's words when he wrote, "The gifts are of various kinds, but the burdens must be borne the way they have been laid upon each person."[14]

Luther encouraged Christians not to renounce or reject their callings. In doing so, he referred primarily to a person's occupation or profession. Obviously, some callings cannot be abandoned or changed. One may refuse to carry out certain responsibilities, but cannot stop being a son, father, and citizen or stop being a daughter, mother, and citizen. Luther *repeatedly* taught that Christians should not abandon their callings. In this regard, he counseled, "[I]t is necessary to observe the rule that everyone should remain in his calling and live content with his gifts."[15] In saying this, Luther emphasized that he did not want Christians to leave one calling for another because of selfish ambition, because they wanted to do what someone else does, because they desired to please another person, or because they longed to do something they believed to be more honorable, comfortable, or profitable. Christians are to stay where God has called them according to their place in life and in keeping with the gifts He has given them.

Luther's admonition, however, did not mean that a change of callings, or aspects of one's calling, is out of the question. Luther himself allowed for the possibility of change. "So it is our responsibility, each in his calling in life, to do all he can to his last breath. We cannot, with clear conscience, leave the place to which God has appointed us, unless we are compelled to do so by force, or unless God clearly shows us through a prophet or some sign that we should do so."[16] We remember that St. Paul urged a slave to become a free man if circumstances permitted (1 Corinthians 7:20–21). For his part, Luther believed all offices should be available to persons qualified for them. He encouraged education to prepare students for offices appropriate for the deployment of their gifts and abilities. This conviction moved Luther to write:

> Look about you at the courts of all the kings and princes, at the cities and the parishes, and see whether they do not contain many striking examples of the fulfillment of this psalm [Psalm 113]. There you will find jurists, doctors, counselors, writers, preachers, who for the most part were poor and who have certainly all attended school, and who by means of the pen have risen to where they are lords—as this psalm says—helping to rule land and people like princes. It is not God's will that only those who are born kings, princes, lords, and nobles should exercise rule and lordship. He wills to have his beggars among them also, lest they think it is nobility of birth rather than God alone who makes lords and rulers.[17]

In his book *God at Work*, Gene Veith explains his understanding of Luther's thought about changing a calling. He concludes:

> While we have a calling in our place of work, we may very well receive another calling to somewhere else. The slave in the text [1 Corinthians 7:20–21] might have the opportunity for freedom. A worker slogging away faithfully in his vocation may get the chance for a better job. Again, the call of God may come through a job offer, a proposal, or an election. Since vocations are multiple and are in the here and now, the calling to be a student might be supplemented by a calling at a fast-food restaurant. Upon graduation, the calling may be to a stock brokerage on Wall Street. In each case, he can be confident in God's purpose for his life and be in a position where he can love and serve his neighbors. At every stage he is leading "the life that the Lord has assigned to him, and to which God has called him."[18]

Just as Scripture does, Luther emphasized that God works through Christians to provide good for others. He elevated the Christian's calling to its high place in God's design when he wrote, "[I]t is God's command that you should do your duty, and *He wants to work through you.* Therefore you must devote yourself to your work and duty with all your strength and attention, and leave the rest to God."[19]

Dr. Luther encouraged Christians to understand how great the Christian life of vocation truly is and assured us of God's forgiveness when sometimes our frailties and weakness of faith interfere with our faithfulness. Here are his words:

> And if I thus remain in Christ, then it is certain that for His sake my vocation, my life, and my works are also acceptable to God and are precious fruits in His sight. And though I myself am still weak in the faith, and though many frailties and sinful lusts still dwell within me and always manifest themselves, this will not be reckoned against me but will be forgiven, provided I do not yield to them, give them free rein, or let myself be torn from faith and from the Vine.[20]

God has surely given great privilege and opportunities to all His people. We are able to serve Him and our neighbors in our daily lives and places. We do not need to look for the extraordinary in life to be of great value to God and others. We need only to be faithful in our callings through which God does good in the lives of others.

Time for New Callings

Having reviewed what Martin Luther says about the Christian calling and its various facets, we are ready to speak of retirement as a God-given opportunity for Christians to receive, from the guidance of God and the strength He gives, new direction in their callings, or places in life, that variously exist within their calling to be a Christian.

Before retirement most retirees have spent a large amount of their time and energy on their professional or occupational calling. At the time of retirement they no longer have their full-time professional or occupational calling. Does this mean they no longer have a calling? By no means! They remain in their vocations as a father, mother, church member, citizen, and so on. Now, however, they can add to that list a calling or callings, provided by the guidance of God, which replace the vocation of a full-time profession or occupation. They have occasion to encounter new ways that permit God to work through them for serving others in love. It is an exciting and challenging time, a time to enter upon a new way or ways opened up by God to make contributions for the enrichment of the lives of others.

What new calling or callings should retirees consider?

That decision certainly depends on where God has led them in life—on their expertise, abilities, experiences, health, and interests. The decision-making process can be an opportunity for them to be led by God to make use of their professional and vocational gifts and experiences in ways other than full-time employment. It is a time, given and directed by God, for them to employ their God-endowed abilities and skills in new ventures that, by God's leading, they identify when they retire and may have wanted to pursue for a long time. For example, today many retirees decide to continue to work at their previous occupations or professions on a part-time basis, pursue additional formal education to enhance their knowledge and skills, explore and employ their hobbies more fully for their benefit and that of others, join in efforts to help the poor and homeless, or spend more time with spouses and children.

Those who have only a modest degree of health and energy also have new callings to pursue. No Christian is ever without a multi-faceted calling. They can focus on prayer, Christian witness in ways available to them, and care for others in person, by correspondence, or by telephone. They may even have a calling simply to rest and patiently endure their infirmities. The possibilities for those healthy and not so healthy are endless.

Most people know far in advance when their retirement will begin. Pre-retirement time provides them with the possibility of considering ways God may want them to redesign components of their callings in retirement. In making decisions, they will prayerfully look to God for guidance and consult the Bible to learn what God has to say about the Christian vocation. In Scripture they will find the suggestive examples of prophets, apostles, and everyday godly people. To assist them in their decision-making, they will find it helpful to consult people who know them well, especially their pastor, family members, colleagues, and friends whom God may use as His instruments. These knowledgeable people very likely have insights and ideas for them to consider concerning how God might want to make the best use of their personal gifts and abilities in their retirement years. Praying and meditating during their decision-making process, people looking forward to years of retirement will trust that the Lord will guide them. Knowing that nothing begun in the name of Jesus is an undertaking begun in vain, they will look to Him to forgive their mistakes and prosper their lives.

When some people retire, they feel at loose ends, and even useless, because so much changes in their daily lives. They no longer have their longtime daily interpersonal relationships, schedules, and activities. They miss the challenges and successes of professional or occupational work. They are not sure how to use their time and how to continue to feel useful and valuable. To a large extent their sense of identity has been bound up with their jobs. It is easy for them to feel unimportant, directionless, and depressed. However, preparations for retirement, like those we have discussed, can help new retirees avoid pitfalls as God works through them and others for the enrichment of their lives and those of other people. This task is to be undertaken in prayer by asking for, and depending on, the guidance of God as He redirects their unique multifaceted calling in life.

Observers of today's retiring adults and those about to retire suggest that perhaps a majority have a heightened interest in vocations that permit them to move from wanting to live successful lives to enjoying lives that focus on significance and leaving a legacy. They also suggest that in former times senior adults required volunteers but now are the source of volunteers. They required caretakers but now are caregivers. In the past, the congregation had one senior adult group and program. Now it fosters multiple senior adult groups and programs. The Christian congregation recognizes that retirees have many interests. They are not simply interested in play but in work, learning, and serving as well as playing.[21]

In their book *Catch the Age Wave*, Win and Charles Arn propose the following set of values that we may find useful to consider. They may well characterize, at least to some degree, many people today who are over 55. They offer the following comments:

People over 55 tend to:

1. Respond to teaching.
2. Be willing to sacrifice personally for a worthy goal or cause.
3. Prefer stability.
4. Resist rapid change.
5. Prefer to associate with those of like beliefs/values.
6. Respect authority.
7. Believe in the value of institutions and are willing to serve to ensure their success/survival.
8. Have a high degree of "loyalty" (marriage, brands, church, employer, institutions, clubs).
9. Consider volunteering as both a privilege and a responsibility.[22]

As we consider the great opportunity for new callings among Christian older adults, I will share also for your consideration the following paragraphs from *Catch the Age Wave*. These authors suggest attitudes and values, also emphasized by other writers, that we might expect among contemporary Christian older adults.

> New seniors do not think of themselves as old or declining. (They would rarely attend a senior citizens group.) They view the future as a time of harvest and renewal rather than the beginning of a cold winter. These people function on new assumptions about living. If retired, they see the gift of new freedom as an opportunity for work, for learning, for service, for growing, and for play. They are focused on the present and the future, not on the past; on serving, not on being served; on involvement, not on disengagement.
>
> New seniors who are Christians recognize this stage of life as an opportunity to serve Christ and His Church, a chance to make a contribution through their experience, their skills, their knowledge, their energy, and the other resources they have developed. Fulfilling these dreams is a motivating challenge.

> New seniors have goals and objectives superimposed on their memories and history. They intend to keep growing and discovering and to join with others of similar mind-set and lifestyle. These people hold the key to a changed view of aging for the church and the entire nation. The church that provides opportunities for older adults to fulfill their dreams and goals will be the church able to reach this rapidly growing generation of Americans.[23]

Our time in history is truly the time when we can emphasize the greatness of the opportunity for older adults, under the guidance of God and by His leading, to reconfigure the content of their callings in life as Christians. They can do much to benefit society, especially those who are in need of their Christlike aid and assistance. Many are ready for the pursuit, eagerly ready.

4 MINISTRY AMONG OLDER ADULTS

MINISTRY TO OLDER ADULTS

As I have already indicated and want to repeat here, I have chosen in this book to speak of ministry *among* older adults rather than talk merely about ministry *to* older adults. This book is interested in ministry *by* and *with* older adults, as well as ministry *to* older adults. From my perspective, ministry *among* older adults embraces ministry *to, by*, and *with* older adults.

Like all of us, older adults need others to minister to them. By God's design, we all have needs that only others can supply. We all require service for spiritual, physical, emotional, and social needs. The ministry, or Christian service, to older adults of which I speak is service provided by both full-time church workers and laypeople, including older adults themselves. It is the service that Jesus makes possible and requires of all His people. In a later chapter, we shall speak more specifically about ways to serve. Now, however, it is imperative for us to affirm the importance of ministry *to* older adults and commit ourselves to doing and facilitating that ministry.

> *When it comes to Christian service, the Lord Jesus is always our teacher, example, and motivation.*

Our service flows from His service to us by which He gave His life as a ransom for us and for all. To His disciples, and that includes us, Jesus said, "[W]hoever would be great among you must be your servant, and whoever would be first among you must be your slave, even as the Son of Man came not to be served but to serve, and to give His life as a ransom for many" (Matthew 20:26b–28).

Jesus, who came to serve, has directed us to look after one another's spiritual well-being. We are to speak the Gospel into one another's lives so we continue to receive and proclaim saving faith in Jesus. Such faith gives comfort, consolation, and strength to meet the fears, challenges, and burdens of each day. Such faith clings to the very power of God to live the newness of our baptismal lives each and every day. Jesus gives us the Gospel through Word and Sacrament for spiritual health and well-being. These means bestow on us the blessings of God that affect every facet of our lives. To the paralytic whom He healed Jesus said, "Take heart, My son; your sins are forgiven" (Matthew 9:2). This is the message by which we all live and need to speak and hear over and over day after day. The message may sound too good to be true, but in this case what may sound too good to be true is most certainly true. As Martin Luther said in his explanation to the Third Article of the Apostles' Creed, "He [God] daily and abundantly forgives all my sins, and the sins of all believers."[1]

Moreover, we remember how Jesus emphasized the importance of feeding the hungry, giving drink to the thirsty, providing shelter for the homeless, and giving clothing to those without clothes. Indeed, He spoke of these acts of Christian service as service done to Himself (Matthew 25:31–40). Older adults have a variety of spiritual, physical, mental, emotional, and social needs. Among their needs we recognize these: a conviction of God's love and forgiveness; a sense of value; loving, supportive, and encouraging relatives and friends; worthwhile activities that enrich their lives and are helpful to others; educational and recreational activities; activities and resources for physical health and well-being; and assistance with many tasks of daily living. Many need special help to deal with specific losses in their lives—the loss of strength and physical attractiveness; the loss of a spouse; the loss of an accustomed way of life at work, at church, and among relatives and friends; the loss of living in their own homes; the loss of income; the loss of friends and relatives through death. Ministry to older adults can and does address itself to serious concerns and brings God's own help to meet their needs.

We have biblical examples of people who ministered to older adults. Jesus ministered to many people older than He was. As He was dying, Jesus ministered to His mother when He directed "the disciple whom He loved" to take care of her as his own mother (John 19:26–27). David played his harp to give relief to King Saul when an evil spirit came upon him (1 Samuel 16:23). Ruth took good care of her mother-in-law, Naomi. At the birth of Jesse, the son of Ruth and Boaz and the father of David, "women said to Naomi, 'Blessed be the LORD, who has not left you this day without a redeemer, and may His name be renowned in Israel! He shall be to you a restorer of life and a nourisher of your old age, for your daughter-in-law who loves you, who is more to you than seven sons, has given birth to him.' " (Ruth 4:14–15). In the Scriptures, we see extended family members caring for each other and honoring older persons. This is in contrast to the isolation of many modern nuclear families and the loneliness that sometimes accompanies old age.

Ministry by Older Adults

A vast number of older adults both want to be of service to others and have much to offer that others need. God works through them to support and enrich the lives of others, including other older adults. What we have said about ministry *to* older adults, we can say about ministry *by* older adults. In fact, there are some kinds of service that older adults may be able to provide better for other senior adults than younger persons. It is because they themselves deal with similar issues and find help through the ministry they seek and receive from God and others.

The ministry by older adults is, of course, by no means limited to ministry for the exclusive benefit of other older adults. Out of the richness of their experiences, abilities, and skills, they have much to offer to people of all ages. Older Christians have learned much they can share with others about living the "ups and downs" of the Christian life. Throughout their lives they have gained valuable knowledge and skills to pass on to others. Also, retired adults likely have more time to minister to others than people who have not yet reached retirement.

We make a serious mistake if we do not involve older adults in ministry. We fail to appreciate the gifts that God has given them and thereby might give through their vocation for the care for others. By undervaluing their gifts, we devalue their lives and diminish the quality of their lives and the lives of others who need what they have to offer. Many adults who are not called upon to minister to others feel unwanted. True, some adults may feel that they do not want to be active as servants and need special encouragement. Others are waiting to be invited to minister, and they feel hurt because no one calls on them for their services. On the other hand, there are always those who take it upon themselves to identify the new calling or callings God wants them to pursue, and they are active in getting involved in various aspects of service to both young and old.

We can readily find biblical examples of ministry by older adults. The older adults Simeon and Anna ministered to others, to Mary and Joseph in the temple, and to citizens of Jerusalem, by their witness to Jesus as the Messiah (Luke 2:25–39). The elderly Elizabeth ministered to Mary when Mary visited her before the birth of Jesus (Luke 1:39–45). The poor widow, whom Jesus praised, cared for others when she put two very small copper coins, all she had to live on, into the temple treasury (Luke 21:1–4). After Jesus healed Peter's mother-in-law, who had a fever, "she rose and began to serve Him" (Matthew 8:14–15).

When St. Paul wrote to Titus, he showed how he believed older people have beneficial ministry to offer. He spoke of how older women can minister to younger women. Paul wrote:

> Older women likewise are to be reverent in behavior, not slanderers or slaves to much wine. They are to teach what is good, and so train the young women to love their husbands and children, to be self-controlled, pure, working at home, kind, and submissive to their own husbands, that the word of God may not be reviled. (Titus 2:3–5)

A biblical example of the fruit of an older person's instruction in the life of a younger person is Lois, the grandmother of Timothy. She shared the Christian faith with her grandson. Paul wrote to Timothy, "I am reminded of your sincere faith, a faith that dwelt first in your grandmother Lois and your mother Eunice and now, I am sure, dwells in you as well" (2 Timothy 1:5). Older adults provide essential ministry to many of all ages.

Ministry among Generations

When we talk about the ministry to and by older adults, it is essential for us to talk about their service both to one another and together to others. This service among generations is called intergenerational ministry, multigenerational ministry, and cross-generational ministry. God has much to say in the Bible about ministry among generations. First of all, we note that He speaks clearly of the service of the older to the younger.

Psalm 145 speaks of an older generation telling of God's greatness to the next generation. While this Psalm may address itself primarily to the teaching role of the head of the family and other God-appointed teachers, the words of the psalmist nonetheless highlight the importance of intergenerational ministry. Thus they serve as wise counsel to all God's people.

> I will extol You, my God and King,
> and bless Your name forever and ever.
> Every day I will bless You
> and praise Your name forever and ever.
> Great is the Lord, and greatly to be praised,
> and His greatness is unsearchable.
>
> One generation shall commend Your works to another,
> and shall declare Your mighty acts.
> On the glorious splendor of Your majesty,
> and on Your wondrous works, I will meditate.
> They shall speak of the might of Your awesome deeds,
> and I will declare Your greatness.
> They shall pour forth the fame of Your abundant goodness
> and shall sing aloud of Your righteousness. (Psalm 145:1–7)

This Psalm speaks of intergenerational service and the exemplary relationship between young and old as the older commend God's works and speak of His majesty to a coming generation.

The next quote, from Psalm 78, clearly speaks of intergenerational ministry. What older adults have learned from their fathers, they are to tell the next generation. They are to share with them the message of God's goodness and greatness that has been passed down by the fathers from an earlier generation. Then, those who receive the fathers' instruction are, in turn, to pass it down to their children.

> Give ear, O my people, to my teaching;
> incline your ears to the words of my mouth!
> I will open my mouth in a parable;
> I will utter dark sayings from of old,
> things that we have heard and known,
> that our fathers have told us.
> We will not hide them from their children,
> but tell to the coming generation
> the glorious deeds of the LORD, and His might,
> and the wonders that He has done.
>
> He established a testimony in Jacob
> and appointed a law in Israel,
> which He commanded our fathers
> to teach to their children,
> that the next generation might know them,
> the children yet unborn,
> and arise and tell them to their children. . . . (Psalm 78:1–6)

As in the case of Psalm 145, Psalm 78 may address itself primarily to the teaching role of the head of the family and other God-appointed teachers; however, the words of the psalmist highlight the necessity and great value of intergenerational ministry among all the people of God.

Moses in his generation instructed parents to impress God's commandments on their children and to talk to their children about them (Deuteronomy 6:6–7). In instituting the Passover observance, Moses said to the people, "And when your children say to you, 'What do you mean by this service?' you shall say, 'It is the sacrifice of the LORD'S Passover, for He passed over the houses of the people of Israel in Egypt, when He struck the Egyptians but spared our houses' " (Exodus 12:26–27). The people of God were to use the Passover celebration to tell their children about the deliverance God provided His people from their slavery in Egypt. They were to pass on the Passover message from generation to generation.

A biblical example of the younger serving the older is found in the Book of Job. When three older men sought to give Job advice about his profound suffering, a younger man by the name of Elihu offered his counsel to them and to Job. He introduced his words affirming that younger people have a service to offer to the older. He said to them,

> I am young in years,
>   and you are aged;
> therefore I was timid and afraid
>   to declare my opinion to you.
> I said, "Let days speak,
>   and many years teach wisdom."
> But it is the spirit in man,
>   the breath of the Almighty, that makes him understand.
> It is not the old who are wise,
>   nor the aged who understand what is right.
> Therefore I say, "Listen to me;
>   let me also declare my opinion." (Job 32:6–10)

In his discourse, Elihu ministered to Job. He pointed the suffering Job, who was seeking to find the meaning of his pain, to God. He told Job that he was ill-advised to rebel against God because God is great in power and justice, and abundant in righteousness (Job 27:32).

We have given attention to the service of older people to the younger and younger people to the older. When we talk about intergenerational ministry, are we able to find biblical examples of the ministry of young and older people together for others? Yes, we have the example of the relationship of St. Paul and St. Timothy. Paul, of course, was an apostle, and Timothy was a young man Paul ordained for the sacred ministry. We need to view their relationship in that light, but, at the same time, their relationship gives us an example of an older adult and a younger adult working together for the good of others.

Timothy joined Paul on his second missionary journey (Acts 16:1). Luke writes that they traveled from town to town and "delivered to them for observance the decisions that had been reached by the apostles and elders who were in Jerusalem" (Acts 16:4). Then, Luke observes, "the churches were strengthened in the faith, and they increased in numbers daily" (Acts 16:5). In turn, Timothy was a co-writer with Paul of the first and second letters to the Thessalonians and of the letter to Philemon (1 Thessalonians 1:1; 2 Thessalonians 2:1; Philemon 1). St. Paul involved Timothy in the ministry of Word and Sacrament, and, sometimes working together, they benefited many others by the proclamation of the Gospel. In them we see two generations working together to enrich the lives of others.

In an earlier time there were probably three generations found in a congregation. But as we enter the twenty-first century, with the life expectancy increasing, we may have at least four generations of people in a Christian congregation. In his 2002 book *One Church, Four Generations*, Gary L. McIntosh, using generally understood terms, speaks of the four generations within the congregation as Builders, Boomers, Busters, and Bridgers. Builders, the get-it-done generation, are those born before 1946 and who today are in their late 50s and older. Boomers, the largest generation, are those born between 1946 and 1964. The Busters, called as such because their generation is smaller than the Boomer generation, are people born between 1965 and 1983. The Bridgers make up the newest generation. Those of this generation are in their early 20s and younger. McIntosh characterizes them as "technologically astute, tolerant of diversity, and superfragmented regarding their preferences."[2] In considering each of these generations, McIntosh points to the uniqueness of each of these generations and urges that we give informed attention to each. You may want to review and evaluate what he has to say.

McIntosh speaks compelling words when he writes that we are always to encourage mutual respect among generations and encourage one generation to value the others. He recommends a seven-step plan that he adapts from Dr. Larry Regenfuss, based on Romans 12:10–18.

Step one: Be devoted to one another in love.

Step two: Give preference to one another in honor.

Step three: Be of the same mind toward one another.

Step four: Do not be haughty in mind.

Step five: Do not be wise in your own estimation.

Step six: Respect what is right in the sight of all people.

Step seven: Be at peace with all people.[3]

God's direction for ministry
among older adults
comes to us as
He reveals His will
for His Church.

5 Direction for Older Adult Ministries

Intentional Ministry

This book does not mean to imply that congregations do not minister among older adults. Where there are members of the congregation who are older adults and where there is Word and Sacrament ministry, ministry to older adults is being carried forward. However, we need to ask if we are doing service among older adults as competently and comprehensively as we should and can be doing. We ought to ask if we are adequately planning for the future when the number of older adults will be much larger than it is now, instead of the congregation just doing business as usual. What we need to avoid is believing that adequate ministry among older adults just happens automatically in the congregation when the congregation "goes about business as usual."

Our responsibility is to take time and opportunity in an intentional program of action to plan and carry out ministry among older adults. We need to periodically evaluate what we are doing and make adjustments as necessary. We must not let such important ministry simply "happen as it will happen" or be satisfied with less than the best that we have to offer.

Goal-Directed Ministry

Intentional ministry calls for goal-directed planning and goal-directed actions. Such ministry involves identifying what goals we want to achieve and deciding how we shall go about reaching the goals. It is important that the goals are worthy, realistic, and achievable and that the ways we go about achieving the goals seem suitable for success. Furthermore, we need to assign tasks to specific persons and assist them as needed so actions take place as planned. These persons, in turn, are to be accountable to the group who is responsible for overseeing ministry among older adults. Finally, it is important to evaluate the progress being made in achieving the designed goals, and then make revisions and additions as advisable to the planning and action processes. We shall discuss concrete ways of implementing such planning in future chapters.

God-Directed Ministry

Those who minister among older adults need both God's direction and assistance for carrying out intentional, goal-directed ministry. Older adults, too, need God's direction and help to carry out their service. Jesus has made it quite clear that we can do nothing of value apart from Him. Jesus told His disciples, "I am the vine; you are the branches. Whoever abides in Me and I in him, he it is that bears much fruit, for apart from Me you can do nothing" (John 15:5).

	Goal-Directed Planning	*Goal-directed Actions*
1)	identify the goal	how to reach the goal
2)	assign tasks	assist as needed
3)	evaluate progress	make revisions and additions

God's direction for ministry among older adults comes to us as He reveals His will for His Church. This means that we are able to shape our Christian callings and go about tasks of Christian service when we recognize what the Church is and what God has called His Church to do. What is the Church? What has God commissioned the Church to do? How does He energize the Church for its mission? When we know the answers to these questions, we are prepared for Christian service.

What is the Church? The New Testament defines the Church as the people of God. All Christians at a particular location and throughout the world are the Church of God. The Church is the people of God; the people of God are His Church. In this Church, perceptible only to faith, there are no hypocrites and unbelievers.

In the institutional Church that is perceptible (visible) to sight, there are hypocrites and unbelievers. However, wherever the Gospel is proclaimed and the Sacraments are rightly administered in the institutional Church, there are true believers who make up the Church identified in the New Testament as the people of God.

The primary confessional document of the Lutheran Church, the Augsburg Confession, biblically and clearly states what the Church is. In Article VII, the Confession states, "It is also taught among us that one holy Christian church will be and remain forever. This is the assembly of all believers among whom the Gospel is preached in its purity and the holy sacraments are administered according to the Gospel."[1] In Article VIII, the document adds, "[A]lthough the Christian church, properly speaking, is nothing else than the assembly of all believers and saints, yet . . . in this life many false Christians, hypocrites, and even open sinners remain among the godly . . . "[2]

By nature we are not the people of God; God makes us His people. As we are born into the world, we are separated from God and His life. Scripture characterizes us as dead in trespasses and sins and under the wrath of God (Ephesians 2:1–3). We daily disobey God and deserve nothing but His present and eternal punishment. But in His great love and undeserved goodness,

> [W]hen the fullness of time had come, God sent forth His Son, born of woman, born under the law, to redeem those who were under the law, so that we might receive adoption as sons. And

> because you are sons, God has sent the Spirit of His Son into our hearts, crying, "Abba! Father!" So you are no longer a slave, but a son, and if a son, then an heir through God. (Galatians 4:4–7)

Jesus, God's own Son who lived among us as a man, has freed us from sin, its punishment and power, and from eternal death and its dread. He has done this by living a life completely obedient to His Father and by His innocent suffering and death on the cross. On the cross, Jesus, the sinless Son of God, traded places with us before God and fully paid the debt we owe God because of our sinfulness and sins. He suffered and died to make good for our disobedient nature and disobedient and destructive actions.

God has designed that through faith in Jesus as the One who saves us, we become His forgiven and renewed people. The following two passages of Scripture make this clear. To Titus, St. Paul wrote, "Jesus Christ . . . gave Himself for us to redeem us from all lawlessness and to purify for Himself a people for his own possession who are zealous for good works" (Titus 2:13–14). Then, to the Christians at Ephesus, Paul wrote, "For by grace you have been saved through faith. And this is not your own doing; it is the gift of God, not a result of works, so that no one may boast. For we are His workmanship, created in Christ Jesus for good works, which God prepared beforehand, that we should walk in them" (Ephesians 2:8–10). It is most certainly true that God "made [Jesus] to be sin who knew no sin, so that in Him we might become the righteousness of God" (2 Corinthians 5:21).

God has special ways of putting us into a saving and life-renewing relationship with Himself through faith. He calls us to Himself, and He creates in us saving faith through the Gospel in Word and in Holy Baptism. St. Paul tells us "faith comes from hearing, and hearing through the word of Christ" (Romans 10:17). Of the blessings of Baptism, Paul wrote to Titus,

> But when the goodness and loving kindness of God our Savior appeared, He saved us, not because of works done by us in righteousness, but according to His own mercy, by the washing of regeneration and renewal of the Holy Spirit, whom He poured out on us richly through Jesus Christ our Savior, so that being

> justified by His grace we might become heirs according to the hope of eternal life. (Titus 3:4–7)

All who are baptized into Jesus Christ and have faith in Him as the Savior from the punishment and power of sin are God's people. We are the people whom God calls His Church, just as Paul assured the Christians in Corinth that they were a Church together with Christians in other places. To them he wrote, "Paul, called by the will of God to be an apostle of Christ Jesus, and our brother Sosthenes, To the church of God that is in Corinth, to those sanctified in Christ Jesus, called to be saints together with all those who in every place call upon the name of our Lord Jesus Christ, both their Lord and ours . . . " (1 Corinthians 1:1–2).

Paul spoke of the Church in a way that is especially appropriate to our topic of ministry to others. He spoke of the Church as the body of Christ. He emphasized that each of us is a member of the body of Christ with special gifts to use in the life and service of God's people. There are three passages from the pen of St. Paul that call for our attention. (1) "For just as the body is one and has many members, and all the members of the body, though many, are one body, so it is with Christ. For in one Spirit we were all baptized into one body—Jews or Greeks, slaves or free—and all were made to drink of one Spirit" (1 Corinthians 12:12–13). (2) "For as in one body we have many members, and the members do not all have the same function, so we, though many, are one body in Christ, and individually members one of another. Having gifts that differ according to the grace given to us, let us use them: if prophecy, in proportion to our faith" (Romans 12:4–6). (3) "To each is given the manifestation of the Spirit for the common good" (1 Corinthians 12:7).

The Church is God's people. But what, we ask, are God's purposes for us? What does God want us to do as His Church? The Bible teaches us that first and foremost God calls us to worship Him as Christian congregations. This worship of God's people gathered together, first of all, acknowledges and celebrates the forgiving and renewing presence of Jesus Christ among His gathered people. It centers in God's Word and Sacraments as He gives them as gifts. Jesus bids us to proclaim, hear, and share His Word and to do with bread and wine what He has commanded us to do.

Among Christian commentators are those who look upon the following New Testament passages as referring to Word and Sacrament worship and its centrality among early Christians. Luke wrote of the congregation at Troas, "On the first day of the week, when we were gathered together to break bread, Paul talked with them" (Acts 20:7). The writer of the letter to the Hebrews directed: "And let us consider how to stir up one another to love and good works, not neglecting to meet together, as is the habit of some . . . " (Hebrews 10:24–25a).

1 But why do we worship? First of all, the Lord calls the baptized together to give them His gifts of forgiveness and His very own life. At the Divine Service He communes with His people. He speaks to us from His Word. He gives us the very body and blood of His Son, Jesus, and an abundant supply of His sin-forgiving love and life-giving Holy Spirit. Everything that goes on in worship flows from these gifts of God.

2 Second, we honor God and offer to Him the sacrifice of praise and thanksgiving in response to His goodness. St. Peter and the writer to the Hebrews teach us that such sacrifice is pleasing to God (1 Peter 2:4–5; Hebrews 13:15). Our thanksgiving includes the rededication of ourselves for Christian living in our callings and the giving of money as an expression of the fuller dedication of our entire selves for the purposes of God. St. Paul encourages us to sacrifice our bodies to God. To the Romans he wrote, "I appeal to you therefore, brothers, by the mercies of God, to present your bodies as a living sacrifice, holy and acceptable to God, which is your spiritual worship" (Romans 12:1).

3 Third, in our worship services we nurture and encourage one another's faith and life in Christ. We speak and sing the Word of God into one another's hearing as St. Paul has directed us to do with the words: "Let the word of Christ dwell in you richly, teaching and admonishing one another in all wisdom, singing psalms and hymns and spiritual songs, with thankfulness in your hearts to God" (Colossians 3:16).

4 Finally, in our worship, as God desires, we pray for all kinds and conditions of people. We recall the words of St. Paul to Timothy, "First of all, then, I urge that supplications, prayers, intercessions, and thanksgivings be made for all people, for kings and all who are in high positions" (1 Timothy 2:1–4).

Now we come to the second of God's purposes for His Church. Just as we nurture one another's faith and life in Christ in worship on the Lord's Day, so God calls us to minister daily to one another as members together of the body of Christ. God calls us to mutual care. He wants us to take care of one another both spiritually and physically (Ephesians 4:11–13, 15; Galatians 6:10; Matthew 25:34–40; James 2:14–17; Acts 2:44–45). Let us be certain of this: In our ministry to one another's needs, we never want to overlook spiritual care. We remember that we have done nothing of eternal importance for people if we care only for their physical, mental, and environmental needs. Yet we recall St. Paul's words, "So then, as we have opportunity, let us do good to everyone, and especially to those who are of the household of faith" (Galatians 6:10). God works through us in our callings to care for one another.

The third mission God gives us is to minister to the world. First, we are to witness to the Gospel of Jesus Christ that people may become His disciples. In turn, as members of the body of Christ, we are called to support the Holy Ministry of Word and Sacraments, and to encourage those who hear the Gospel to be baptized (Matthew 28:19–20). Aquila and his wife Priscilla are examples for us. They were laypeople St. Paul called his fellow workers. Paul writes they "risked their necks for my life, to whom not only I give thanks but all the churches of the Gentiles give thanks as well" (Romans 16:3). In Ephesus they invited Apollos into their home "and explained to him the way of God more accurately" (Acts 18:26). Apollos, in turn, became a powerful witness to Jesus Christ. St. Paul says the same for the members of the Christian congregation in Thessalonica. He wrote to them, "[T]he word of the Lord sounded forth from you in Macedonia and Achaia, but your faith in God has gone forth everywhere" (1 Thessalonians 1:8).

In our service to the world we are also called to provide holistic care for people just as Jesus did (Matthew 9:35–38). While we always give priority to looking after people's spiritual needs, we do not neglect caring for their physical needs. Often only when we minister to people's physical needs do they come to trust us to care for them spiritually. But whether or not they immediately hear and believe the saving news of Jesus, we still care for the sick, feed the hungry, give drink to the thirsty, visit those in prison, and clothe those who need clothing. We seek to do what Jesus Christ did and to be Christ to people as He has instructed us (Matthew 9:35; Matthew 9:36–38).

God Himself ministers to us through Word and Sacrament.

6 God's Resources for Older Adult Ministries

Our purposes as a Church are to receive God's saving and life-changing gifts in worship, to respond with praise and thanksgiving, to care for one another spiritually and physically, and to minister to the spiritual and physical needs of people outside the Church. These tasks are formidable ones, but God in His goodness gives us the life of the Holy Spirit to do His will and His work through the means He has chosen.

Week by week we receive God's enablement when we gather as God's baptized people for worship on the Lord's Day. God Himself ministers to us through Word and Sacrament. Through these means He sustains and strengthens our faith in Jesus as our Savior, and fosters the work of the Holy Spirit within us. The Holy Spirit, who is the author and giver of life, continually renews our lives to glorify God and serve others in our Christian callings. To summarize, in worship God gives us forgiveness and new life, and thereby prepares us to go forth to live a life that itself is daily worship through our vocation or calling. What we do in each of our callings is truly worship, even though it is different than Sunday morning worship.

. . . the Good News about Jesus Christ, is the very heart of our lives

The daily life we live as Christians is a life that glorifies, thanks, pleases, and serves God. Our daily service to God is manifested through love for our neighbor. He strengthens us to care for one another spiritually and physically, and to care for the spiritual and physical needs of people outside the church. Our new life in Christ is energized each Lord's Day by the Gospel of Jesus Christ in the Word and the Sacrament of the Lord's Supper. In turn, God daily enriches this life as each day we remember our Baptism and the gifts of the Lord's Supper, and as we daily ponder the good news about Jesus Christ. The life we live as Christians is often called the sacramental life because we daily live out the riches of our Baptism and the weekly celebration of the Holy Communion with Word and Sacrament.

We cannot emphasize enough that the Gospel, the Good News about Jesus Christ, is the very heart of our lives. This Gospel word is the power of God to salvation and the power that has brought us new life. St. Paul spoke of the saving power of the Gospel in his letter to the Roman Christians. He wrote, "For I am not ashamed of the gospel, for it is the power of God for salvation to everyone who believes, to the Jew first and also to the Greek" (Romans 1:16). St. Peter also testified to the saving power of the Gospel: "[Y]ou have been born again, not of perishable seed but of imperishable, through the living and abiding word of God" (1 Peter 1:23). In his letter to Titus, St. Paul spoke of the life-changing vigor of the message of the saving and teaching grace of God.

> For the grace of God has appeared, bringing salvation for all people, training us to renounce ungodliness and worldly passions, and to live self-controlled, upright, and godly lives in the present age, waiting for our blessed hope, the appearing of the glory of our great God and Savior Jesus Christ, who gave himself for us to redeem us from all lawlessness and to purify for

himself a people for his own possession who are zealous for good works (Titus 2:11–14).

The Gospel that saves and renews us also works in our lives through the water of Holy Baptism to include us among the forgiven and transformed people of God. St. Paul wrote to Titus about the wonders of Baptism. He told Titus,

> But when the goodness and loving kindness of God our Savior appeared, He saved us, not because of works done by us in righteousness, but according to His own mercy, by the washing of regeneration and renewal of the Holy Spirit, whom He poured out on us richly through Jesus Christ our Savior, so that being justified by His grace we might become heirs according to the hope of eternal life. (Titus 3:4–7)

To the words of St. Paul to Titus we can add the words Paul wrote to the Corinthians about baptism, "For just as the body is one and has many members, and all the members of the body, though many, are one body, so it is with Christ. For in one Spirit we were all baptized into one body—Jews or Greeks, slaves or free—and all were made to drink of one Spirit" (1 Corinthians 12:12–13). Truly, as St. Peter says, baptism saves us (1 Peter 3:21).

Just as it works in Baptism, so the Gospel is at work in the Lord's Supper. The Holy Meal is pure strengthening, reassuring, and life-changing Gospel. In this sacred meal we share together in the body of Christ and in the blood of Christ. He gives Himself to us in His body and blood to convey to us the benefits of the giving of His body and the shedding of His blood on Calvary's cross. The Lord's Supper brings Calvary and all of the benefits of the death of Jesus right into our lives today. The years that separate us from Calvary vanish, and Calvary becomes present for us in the here and now. Consider these words of St. Paul: "The cup of blessing that we bless, is it not a participation [sharing together] in the blood of Christ? The bread that we break, is it not a participation [sharing together] in the body of Christ?" (1 Corinthians 10:16). Paul's words remind us that the Sacrament of the Lord's Supper is also called the Eucharist, the Thanksgiving, and the Holy Communion, the holy sharing together in the Body and Blood of Jesus.

The Gospel that brought us to faith in Jesus and to renewal of life is the same Gospel that sustains and strengthens our faith and continually renews our lives to live according to God's will. It is through this Gospel that God daily enables us to will and do His good pleasure. To be sure, our faith and life in Jesus Christ daily need to be nourished and enlarged. There are parts of our willing and thinking that are not yet under the control of the Holy Spirit. They continually seek to erode our faith and diminish the quality of our new lives in Christ. We are not perfect and cannot be perfect on this side of heaven. We recognize this just as St. Paul did. Yet we look to Jesus for forgiveness and for *strength* in Christian living. Like St. Paul, we know that we, too, often do the evil we do not want to do and do not do the good we want to do, but we count on God who gives us the victory through our Lord Jesus Christ (Romans 7:21–25).

We count on God through the thick and thin of life. He forgives our sins, strengthens our faith, and renews our lives as daily we return to our Baptism through repentance, our sorrow for sins and our turning to God in faith. Our old sinful self is put to death and the new person in Christ arises again and again to wage war against the evil within us and around us. It comes forth to make it possible for us to live the life that is the worship of God, to serve others with God's help, and to rejoice in every advance in our Christian callings.

Everything that we have to say about new life in Christ has meaning for ministry among older adults as they and we seek to serve others in our callings and live the worship-life generated in us daily by the Gospel.

7 Ways of Ministry among Older Adults: Worship, Fellowship, and Stewardship

Introductory Remarks

The time has now come for us to consider ideas for specific ways to minister among older adults. These suggestions have their basis in our study of the nature of the Church and God's purposes for the Church. This study will shape the selection of possible routes of action as we consider ways to minister among older adults. Suggestions offered intend to present possibilities for both ministry *to* older adults and *by* older adults. All suggestions involve ministry *with* older adults as we minister *among* them.

Almost exclusively, suggestions for ministry *to* and ministry *by* older adults given in this section of the book are worded as recommendations for ministry *to* older adults. In most cases the suggestions for ministry *to* older adults contain ideas also for ministry *by* older adults. Conversely, when certain ideas are worded to relate primarily to ministry *by* older adults, these recommendations often also point out ways *to serve* older adults.

By providing one list, rather than two, I have sought to eliminate repetition that would occur by the presentation of both *to* and *by* lists. However, you may find some ideas in one category, such as worship, repeated in another category, sometimes in different words. The functions of the church are not isolated from one another. Therefore, a ministry suggestion might apply to more than one category.

In terms of benefits received, it makes little or no difference whether an older adult is served or serves. All acts of Christian service glorify God and benefit both the giver and the receiver. Congregations are encouraged to choose among the suggestions and how to use them and also to add their own recommendations based on congregational resources and needs.

Earlier we identified the purposes or functions of the Church in broad strokes as worship, mutual care, and outreach into the world. These functions have also related and included components that we will consider in order to fill out our vision of God's will for His Church. In identifying ways of doing ministry among older adults, we will explore possibilities that include worship in congregational and home-bound settings, fellowship, stewardship, and spiritual and physical care for fellow Christians and for non-Christians. We will look upon these topics as presenting a more comprehensive view of the Church's functions, a view that is rooted in, and flows from, our biblical exploration of the nature and purposes of the Church in chapter 5.

In my presentation that follows, I have placed fellowship and stewardship together with worship because they are uniquely associated with worship. In very special ways fellowship and stewardship originate in and flow from worship. In worship Jesus calls us together as His Holy Body. Gathered together around His Word and Holy Supper, we have sublime fellowship with Him and with one another as members of His Body. Jesus shares His love and life with us, and we nurture and encourage one another's Christian faith and life. In turn, such sharing with one another in worship, generated by Jesus and His love through His Word and Sacrament, is the source for all Christian fellowship, our sharing together in our daily lives. Fellowship is characterized by sharing and caring because we are members together in the body of Christ.

Also in worship *we* respond to God's great goodness to and for us by offering to Him our sacrifice of praise and thanksgiving and our gifts of money. These gifts of praise and money in response to God's mercy most certainly represent and include the rededication enjoined by St. Paul in Romans 12. Such rededication in worship, enabled by the love and life that God gives us, is expressed in our stewardship of all of life.

Worship

We now begin with our consideration of worship that we discussed at length in chapter 5. We will talk about congregational worship, but we will also include homebound worship as an extension of the congregational worship of God's people that takes place on the Lord's Day and other holy days. As indicated earlier, the following suggestions are recommendations intended to be used for ministry both *to* older adults and *by* older adults.

Congregational Worship

1. Include one or more older adults as members of the worship committee to express their age group's needs and interests.
2. Involve older adults in worship as appropriate. For example, they can serve as readers, ushers, greeters, Communion assistants, altar guild members, musicians, and choir singers. They can create liturgical art and banners for worship services and assist with the preparation of worship folders.
3. During announcements and prayers in the worship service, recognize couples married for a particular length of years, such as 50 years.

4. Recognize and honor the oldest baptized member(s) on a selected Sunday.
5. On Confirmation Sunday recognize confirmands' grandparents, as well as their parents, as those who have the primary responsibility for children's catechetical instruction.
6. Hold a special Senior Sunday. Provide transportation to and from the church. Perhaps provide for a meal after the service. Enlist the help of persons who are willing to use their cars for transportation.
7. Accommodate older adults who prefer morning or afternoon services on special occasions, such as Ash Wednesday, Good Friday, and Ascension Day.
8. Plan special services at church for homebound and nursing home residents who cannot normally participate in worship at church on Sunday. Provide transportation and have a time, perhaps with a meal, after the service to allow them to get to know each other better. Many members of the congregation will gladly make their cars and vans available.
9. Help those with hearing loss by providing an effective sound system. Place someone in charge of the system at each service or event who is trained for the task.
10. The worship leader should speak slowly, distinctly, and with acceptable volume. Church musicians should be considerate of those using hearing aids.
11. Help those with vision impairments by printing the entire order of service and hymns, also in large print, and/or by using orders of worship and hymns that are familiar to older worshipers.
12. Make available some large print hymnals and Bibles.
13. Certain colors of ink and paper create reading problems for those with vision impairments, regardless of age. These include dark colors such as red and purple.
14. Provide adequate lighting in all church and school facilities. Evaluate whether lights should be dimmed during the sermon or presentations.

15. Mount bulletin boards at an appropriate height for those with bifocals or in wheelchairs.
16. Alleviate mobility problems by installing elevators, chairlifts, or adequate ramps. Provide for both temporary and permanent handicapped parking areas that are sufficiently wide and close to the entrance of the building. Consider reserved parking for those who are temporarily handicapped.
17. Accommodate and make wheelchairs available.
18. Review worship practice to ensure that long periods of standing or sitting do not cause discomfort for the worshipers. Pew cushions or available individual cushions are helpful for many.
19. Make available transportation to and from services. Consider using car or van transportation provided by members and others rather than more expensive modes of transportation that also may present liability problems.
20. In terms of some people's cognitive loss, familiar hymns, Scripture readings, and prayers can be helpful.
21. Worship leaders must set a supportive and encouraging tone of acceptance for those with impairments. Every congregation, large or small, can be user friendly.

Homebound Worship

Worship for the homebound is an extension of the congregation's celebration of the Lord's Supper with Word and Sacrament. Thus we look at ways to implement this ministry. Here are some recommendations.

1. Assist pastors in taking the Word and Sacrament of Holy Communion to those who are homebound, reminding them that their celebration of the Lord's Supper is a part of the fellowship of the congregation gathered around the altar on the Lord's Day and holy days. Help them to understand that the church is where the Word and Sacraments are present and that they are in fellowship with the whole Church in the homebound service.

2. Utilize audio tape recorders and camcorders to record worship services and see to it that the homebound receive these worship resources. When possible, stay with the homebound while they listen or view. Many will likely appreciate your presence and may need your assistance.
3. Assist the pastor in providing worship services, when it is appropriate, at retirement and nursing homes for those who cannot participate, or participate regularly, in congregational worship.
4. Provide daily devotional booklets, such as *Portals of Prayer* and *Strength for the Day* from Concordia Publishing House.
5. Work with the homebound to develop the types of devotions or orders of service most valuable to them.
6. Read devotional materials to homebound persons who, for a variety of reasons, may be unable to read the materials.
7. Develop a resource library with appropriate materials for the homebound and frail elderly. Publicize the availability of the materials and make it convenient for the homebound to receive and to return the materials.
8. Provide the opportunity for the homebound to convey recorded messages to the church administration, older adult meetings, etc.
9. Provide suggested Bible verses and hymn verses for homebound persons to ponder, perhaps also to memorize each day.
10. Give the homebound appropriate prayers for a variety of occasions.
11. Give the homebound names of people for whom they can pray.
12. Make special home worship helps available, especially for times such as Advent, Lent, and Thanksgiving Day.
13. Provide transportation to worship services for nursing home residents who are sometimes able to be out and about. Use available cars and vans.

14. Encourage homebound persons, in ways that may be available to them, to check on the well-being of other homebound persons.
15. Contact older adults, and other members, too, when they are absent from worship.

Fellowship

The word *fellowship* as used among Christians means people sharing together or sharing with one another. Fellowship is one of God's greatest gifts to His people. God does not leave us alone in life; He places us in His family, the Church. The Church, as we have discovered, is the fellowship of God's people created and sustained by God's Word and Sacraments. By God's design, we receive God's bounty, and then enrich one another's lives by supporting and encouraging one another and sharing many good things with others as they share with us. Christian fellowship has many facets with the sharing of God's Word and Sacraments at its heart and center.

St. Paul talks about the fellowship aspect of worship when he speaks of the Lord's Supper as a sharing together in the body of Christ and a sharing together in the blood of Christ. He also commented, "Because there is one bread, we who are many are one body, for we all partake of the one bread" (1 Corinthians 10:17). God's Word calls us to affirm that the heart and soul of fellowship among the people of God is congregational worship and recognize that our sharing in worship continues in sharing together in our daily lives.

A biblical example of fellowship in worship and in daily living among Christians is found in the life of the Christian congregation brought into being by God on the day of Pentecost in the city of Jerusalem. The early Christians certainly shared together and shared with one another. Of these early Christians, Luke wrote words that describe their Word and Sacrament worship life: "[T]hey devoted themselves to the apostles' teaching and fellowship, to the breaking of bread and the prayers" (Acts 2:42). Then, Luke went on to describe the fellowship, or sharing with one another, of those early Christians that flowed from their Word and Sacrament worship. "And all who believed were together and had all things in common. And they were selling their possessions and belongings and distributing the proceeds to all, as any had need. And day by day, attending the temple together and breaking bread in their homes, they received their food with glad and generous hearts, praising God and having favor with all the people. And the Lord added to their number day by day those who were being saved" (Acts 2:44–47).

The early Christians in Jerusalem lived a life of service that extended from their worship services. They were together and had everything in common. Those who were rich with this world's goods sold possessions and expressed their love of Christ by giving money to everyone in need. These Christians expressed and furthered the life of sharing together by eating meals together. They had glad hearts when they were together.

No doubt, the more the early Christians shared together in everyday events and activities the more they came to know each other better and established closer interpersonal relationships. Their everyday activities enabled them to recognize the needs of others. These activities outfitted them better to nurture one another's Christian faith and life. They used their interpersonal events as God-given opportunities to serve and edify one another.

Today we also have many opportunities to serve our Lord apart from our public worship services. We share our financial resources, eat together, and share in many other ways made available to us in the twenty-first century. We enjoy one another and gladden one another's hearts when we do God-approved things together. These times enable us to become acquainted with one another's joys and sorrows and give us opportunities to use our times together to caution, strengthen, and encourage one another, so our relationships with Jesus and His people become stronger. This is why many of our suggestions for fellowship have to do with everyday activities we share together. They are living out the life to which God called us as members of the body of Christ. The following, then, are suggestions for enriching our lives and our friendships for our mutual benefit.

1. Develop programs to assimilate new members of all ages into the active life of the congregation.
2. Initiate Bible study groups around God's Word both at church and in homes.
3. Demonstrate concern for each other through care groups

who pray for people and then show their love by taking care of their needs.

4. Organize senior groups.
5. Find leaders to coordinate activities for various purposes.
6. Develop an ongoing program where individuals will serve for a year as a special friend to a nursing home resident or homebound person.
7. Offer older adults opportunities to become involved in care programs, such as Stephen Ministries (www.stephenministries.org) and hospice programs.
8. Assign an older adult to be a "secret pal" to a Sunday School student. At "rally day" secret pals can share their identities.
9. Discover older people's wants by using a "volunteer and needs survey."
10. Encourage the elders of the congregation who make home visits to be sensitive to the needs of older adults
11. Initiate special interest groups for golfing, traveling, camping, fishing, and other hobbies.
12. Provide educational trips to historic places, etc.
13. Sponsor cultural outings to plays, symphony concerts, etc.
14. Organize a quilters group.
15. Recommend continuing education programs sponsored by community schools.
16. Have older adults compile an "Older Adult Yearbook" each year that includes articles and photographs about the previous year's activities.
17. Encourage older adults to arrange a phone chain to announce matters important to their age groups and the entire congregation.
18. Look into Elderhostel and Luther Hostel programs that provide educational courses at various colleges, universities, and seminaries. (See Appendix B)

19. Inquire about district older adult gatherings or sponsor such events.
20. Check out Lutheran camps for senior events.
21. Use the resources of the Association of Lutheran Older Adults (www.aloaserves.org).
22. Contact Thrivent for information about possible funding for group activities (www.thrivent.com).
23. Prepare a periodic newsletter for older adults by older adults.
24. Ask older members to serve refreshments for congregational meetings and activities.
25. Create a photo directory with pictures and information about each older adult.

Stewardship

Christian stewardship belongs with our discussion of worship because in Word and Sacrament worship we weekly rededicate ourselves and all that we are and have to God. In the service of worship, our money offerings are a part of our rededication and symbol of the totality of our dedication. This is the kind of dedication of which St. Paul speaks: "I appeal to you therefore, brothers, by the mercies of God, to present your bodies as a living sacrifice, holy and acceptable to God, which is your spiritual worship" (Romans 12:1).

As St. Paul says, we offer ourselves as living sacrifices to God in response to the mercies of God. These are His mercies bestowed on us in Christ, our Lord, through Word and Sacrament. They include forgiveness of sins and new life in Christ. This new life in Christ enables us to live the kind of life described by St. Paul in his letter to the Romans. By our baptism into the death and resurrection of Jesus Christ, Jesus enables us to yield ourselves to righteous living in our struggle against the sin that remains in our lives as long as we live earthly lives. Like St. Paul we find sin still living in us (Romans 7:20). But, at the same time, we have the God-given capacity to do what St. Paul enjoins:

> So you also must consider yourselves dead to sin and alive to God in Christ Jesus. Let not sin therefore reign in your mortal bodies, to make you obey their passions. Do not present your members to sin as instruments for unrighteousness, but present yourselves to God as those who have been brought from death to life, and your members to God as instruments for righteousness. For sin will have no dominion over you, since you are not under law but under grace. (Romans 6:11–14)

Christian stewardship is another way of talking about the use of our time, our abilities, our energy, and our money faithfully to fulfill our calling in all its facets. We minister among older adults to enable them to be faithful stewards of God's gifts to them in their God-directed callings as Christians. The following are some ideas for this ministry.

1. Include older adults on the stewardship committee.
2. Organize an older adult "think tank" to suggest meaningful congregational stewardship programs.
3. Encourage older adults in their feelings of personal worth as those who are baptized into the death and resurrection of Jesus Christ (Romans 6) and who are clothed with Christ (Galatians 3:27). Assist them in identifying and using their particular gifts and abilities.
4. Encourage other older adults to serve as role models for both young and old in the matter of stewardship.
5. Consider involvement of older adults in activities to preserve resources and the environment.
6. Assist the congregation in presenting materials and programs to encourage individuals to be good stewards of their money, time, and talents.
7. Help older adults plan their retirement years. Start early and help retirees look to God for His leading in the reshaping of the contents of their calling for expanded service. Local colleges and continuing education programs often teach retirement planning. Fraternal insurance organizations frequently offer helpful materials.

8. Celebrate older adults' retirement as an opportunity for new service as God guides the reconfiguration of their various callings.
9. Present specific short-term opportunities for Christian service activities in the congregation, community, and wider church context.
10. Assist retirees to practice good stewardship of their time. This may be their first chance to control their own schedules and choose how they use their time.
11. Help retirees practice good stewardship of their money, abilities, and energy, as well as the use of their time.
12. Encourage married couples to plan for the financial realities after the death of a spouse.
13. Promote older adult membership on all congregational boards and committees.
14. If older adults have been serving on the boards of the church and desire to be relieved of their duties, ask them to serve as mentors for new board members.
15. Offer opportunities for discussions regarding living wills, the durable power of attorney, and ethical issues, such as the use of life-support systems and organ donations.
16. Encourage the use of wills, living trusts, and other planned giving instruments.
17. Provide information on Medicare, Medicaid, home health care services, nursing homes, long-term health insurance, financial assistance, and reverse mortgages on homes.
18. Publicize a "wish list" for staffing and equipment needs in order to continue and expand the service of the congregation in this area.
19. Assist those who live on a limited income. Share information about federal/state assistance programs. If possible, provide the necessary help needed to make applications for assistance.

20. Encourage retirees to evaluate the potential of a new vocation in a Christian service position, finding ways to use their professional/career experience as a church and community volunteer.
21. Assist older persons to establish a proper balance between leisure and service.
22. Develop an "if the Lord wills" plan for the next few years of life.

The spiritual care we provide for one another as Christians emerges . . .

8 Ways of Ministry among Older Adults: Care for Others

Spiritual Care for Fellow Christians

In His design for the Church, God wants His people to provide spiritual care for fellow Christians and for people still outside the Church. The spiritual care we provide for one another as Christians emerges from our Word and Sacrament worship and is closely bound to the study of the Bible and the speaking of biblical truths, especially the Good News about Jesus Christ, to one another as we live out our Christian lives together. We are concerned that each of us grows up in Christ and becomes a mature Christian. St. Paul has this to say: "[S]peaking the truth in love, we are to grow up in every way into Him who is the head, into Christ" (Ephesians 4:15). Of the use of God's Word, St. Peter wrote, "Like newborn infants, long for the pure spiritual milk, that by it you may grow up to salvation" (1 Peter 2:2). To Timothy St. Paul addressed these words: "All Scripture is breathed out by God and profitable for teaching, for reproof, for correction, and for training in righteousness, that the man of God may be competent, equipped for every good work" (2 Timothy 3:16–17).

The following suggestions are intended to be helpful in facilitating spiritual care among older adult Christians.

1. Have an older adult (or older adults) serve on the education committee.
2. Provide a variety of Bible study opportunities for older adults, especially short-term study opportunities. In all Bible study situations, the time, place, number, and length of sessions are important to an older person. Consider accessibility, lighting, and acoustics, as well as available transportation.
3. Consider a yearlong Bible overview for those who do not plan extended vacations. Longer Bible study courses give older persons opportunity to discuss various books or particular chapters of the Bible in detail.
4. Offer issue-oriented Bible study that provides the opportunity for older adults to discuss many subjects that interest them. The group, in consultation with the pastor, can help determine the issues they wish to study.
5. Offer study of topics on retirement planning, such as attitudes, housing, use of time, opportunities for Christian service, financial matters, legal affairs, and other issues. The study of such topics provides excellent opportunities to plan retirement from a Christian perspective.
6. Make use of materials and topics dealing with the myths about normal aging.
7. Call upon Christian professionals to speak to older adults on ethical issues, such as use of life support systems, living wills, euthanasia, hospice services, and similar subjects.
8. Use staff persons of Lutheran agencies and similar organi-

zations to discuss family life, which can include grandparenting, older adults relating to adult children, neglect and abuse, and other pertinent subjects.

9. Create opportunities for young and old to study the Scriptures together.
10. Use libraries that offer quarterly newsletters from the Elderhostel, an educational program for older adults who want to continue to expand their horizons and develop new interests. (See Appendix B)
11. Provide educational experiences for older adults by referring them to available church and community resources.
12. Initiate support groups for older members to work on their concerns with one another under the guidance of Scripture.
13. Facilitate support groups for senior members to encourage and assist one another in their spiritual development.
14. Invite older adults to share their spiritual growth experiences when a Christian day school class studies certain historic events.
15. Assist older adults to initiate, and participate in, the recording of the congregation's oral and written history. Make documents, tape recordings, pictures, and videos available through the church library.
16. Engage older adults in the development or expansion of the church library. Encourage them to include books, videos, tapes, sight-saving print books, and devotional materials valuable to older adults. Develop a delivery and pick-up service for the homebound. Perhaps the system can work with the delivery of worship service recordings.
17. Enlist older adults to be teachers of Sunday School classes, Bible study groups, and Vacation Bible School.
18. Encourage older adults to serve as mentors for confirmation class members.
19. Interest older adults in serving as a tutor or mentor in various educational areas, both Christian and secular.

Spiritual Care for Non-Christians

Christians give spiritual care to people still outside the church. We do this by witnessing to them about God's Law and Gospel. We help non-Christians understand their sinfulness and their need for a Savior. We tell them the Good News of what Jesus Christ has done and continues to do for us, and what He has done and can do for them. Our goal is to make it possible for the Holy Spirit to work in their lives through the Word of God. We witness so the Holy Spirit might bring them into a saving relationship with God through faith in Jesus as Savior and make them disciples of Jesus and members of His church through baptism. We recall the words of St. Peter, "[Y]ou are a chosen race, a royal priesthood, a holy nation, a people for His own possession, that you may proclaim the excellencies of Him who called you out of darkness into His marvelous light" (1 Peter 2:9).

Declaring our Savior's wonderful deeds is to continue throughout our lifetime, whether we live a few years or a century. As we journey through different phases of life, our experiences as Christians help us to share the Gospel with others. Many older Christians like learning new methods of sharing the Gospel. Retirees have time to be good listeners and to share God's Word. They find it fulfilling to be involved in spiritual care to people of the world.

Some suggestions for congregations and older adults are as follows:

1. Include older adults on the congregation's evangelism committee.
2. Encourage the evangelism committee to review the congregation's witness training to be certain resources are provided for the unique role of older adults.
3. Provide older adults with witness opportunities.
4. Develop tapes and send appropriate materials to the homebound to help them share the Gospel with their visitors.
5. Visit new residents in the community and new residents at nursing homes to share the Gospel.
6. Develop programs for participants, young and old, to demonstrate Christlike caring for others.
7. Encourage older adults to share with others how their

Christian faith has sustained them during their life, especially in times of bereavement, loneliness, and other crisis times.

8. Involve older people in training sessions on personal witnessing.
9. If older adult Christians live in a residence for other older adults, encourage and equip them to conduct Bible studies for all residents.
10. Enlist older persons to visit unchurched people and show sensitivity to their needs. Encourage them to be good listeners, demonstrate concern, and speak the Gospel.
11. Lead older adults to join in community activities that provide Christian service.
12. Assist older adults to become advocates for those who are oppressed or neglected in the community and to look to the pastor for guidance in this endeavor.
13. If older adults are creative in arts and crafts, use them to share the Gospel message by using their unique talents.
14. Inquire about "Harvesters for Christ," a program designed for persons who have compassion for the unchurched and are willing to give a block of time to serve in congregations throughout the larger church. For more information consult with The Lutheran Church—Missouri Synod District and Congregational Services—Outreach Ministry (www.lcms.org), 1-800-248-1930, ext. 1287.

Physical Care for Christians and Non-Christians

God calls all Christians, young and old, to be channels of His love and care both for people of the church and people of the world. God calls us to this task as we live out our callings day by day.

God's love for both people is most appropriately channeled through us when we serve people at their points of need. Sometimes we accomplish this by what we say and do; at other times we do this by finding others who can respond appropriately. By keeping our ears and eyes open, we can hear and see those who are hurting and discover opportunities to respond creatively.

Opportunities for Christian service do not always happen spontaneously; it may be necessary to intentionally search out situations in which to offer service, to provide both daily living care and health care.

Daily Living Care

Because older adults have many different experiences, they offer many kinds of service in the name of Jesus. Many, who do not volunteer, want to be asked to use their spiritual gifts, the accumulated knowledge of their professional lives, and their new gift of time. They will find great satisfaction in providing practical help to those who need their God-given abilities, experience, and knowledge.

Some possibilities for providing care for daily needs are noted below.

1. Include older adults as members of the committee responsible for giving care for people's daily living needs.
2. Provide a central phone number and contact person who has resources for those who need help offered by the congregation or community agencies.
3. Designate an individual to be an advocate for older adults.
4. Among older adults develop a talent bank of volunteers. Be sure to use those who offer their services.
5. Designate certain handicapped-accessible rooms for church groups and community activities.
6. Provide a respite service for families who care full-time for a homebound family member.
7. Use members' professional skills, such as nurses, counselors, carpenters, accountants, lawyers, etc., to assist others. Consider the possibility of having a parish nurse. Help people with home repairs and yard care.
8. Adopt a "servant event" and involve older adults.
9. Assist people of all ages who need transportation.
10. Develop and distribute a list of older adult community services and activities.

11. Develop a bulletin board display of available community services for older persons.

12. Encourage senior individuals to develop skills in visitation and support services through Stephen Ministries (www.stephenministries.com).

13. Investigate the need for an adult day care center.

14. Use the resources of the Area Agency on Aging, the United Way, and other service organizations to become acquainted with community projects and to learn how congregation members may become involved in God-pleasing ways.

15. Confer with hospital social workers. They often need volunteers to look in on individuals for a few days after they return home from an illness or surgery.

16. Keep homebound people up-to-date with appropriate, current material that identifies free community services.

17. Offer your church facility as a place for support group meetings.

18. Provide services at nursing homes, hospitals, clinics, etc. A church van and/or individuals' cars might transport volunteers to a nursing home to serve as "feeders" at the noon meal.

19. Participate in developing a community program for older adults modeled after the Shepherd's Centers of America (www.shepherdcenter.org).

20. Provide parenting classes for grandparents. An increasing number have the full responsibility for raising their grandchildren.

21. Encourage involvement in recycling programs. If sponsored by the community, support them; if not sponsored, encourage starting them.

22. Explore and recommend service programs on a national level that may interest some older people.

23. Investigate and publicize caring possibilities, such as assisting in building homes through Habitat for Humanity (www.habitat.org).

24. Contact the Board for Human Care of The Lutheran Church—Missouri Synod for assistance and information on caring for people.

25. Encourage and enable older adults to:

    - Serve on the congregation's human care committee.
    - Send congregational newsletters, birthday, and baptismal anniversary cards, etc., to older adults, especially the homebound.
    - Serve as special greeters during a "coffee hour" after a worship service, deliver tapes and videos to the homebound, phone visitors later in the week, rearrange altar flowers and deliver them to appropriate people.
    - Keep in touch with frail and homebound persons, especially those who live alone, by personal visits and/or frequent telephone calls.
    - Be willing to serve on state committees working with older adult issues and to make Christian contributions.
    - Collect food and provide a food pantry for needy persons.
    - Gather good, usable clothing and distribute clothes to the needy.
    - Host dinners and programs for older adults.
    - Provide educational programs for older adults that have to do with daily care.
    - Work with community programs that serve people in need, especially the elderly.
    - Provide people with needed transportation.
    - Help people with home repairs and yard work.

Health Care

Health care for fellow Christians and non-Christians is certainly an aspect of daily living care but significant enough to be given special consideration.

Christians recognize life as God's gift redeemed by Jesus Christ. In the strength of the Holy Spirit, Christians strive to enhance physical, mental, and emotional health as gifts of God to be treasured and cared for. With Luther in his Small Catechism we confess, "I believe that God has created me and all that exists; that he has given me and still sustains my body and soul, all my limbs and senses, my reason and all the faculties of my mind."[1] We acknowledge God as our Creator and recognize that our whole being is a gift and sacred trust from Him.

Today people place great emphasis on total health. Exercise is "in," proper diet is a common topic, and people take part in health screenings. All this allows people to be healthier, feel better, and live fuller lives. We Christians seek to care for our bodies as God's gift.

Health and wellness, for many years, have been identified almost exclusively with the medical profession and hospitals. This wasn't always true. The church, following the example of Jesus' healing ministry, led in caring for the whole person. Health and healing are appropriate issues for attention by young and old as we care for the whole person, both spiritually and physically.

The older membership of the congregation is reaching large numbers that call for the congregation to identify and address the health needs of this population. We need especially to be aware of people's needs during their periods of transition. In the developmental stages of life, the transition is to larger horizons and challenges. However, the reverse appears true of transitions in the life of the older adult. Horizons and opportunities seem to shrink with predictable risks to the total well-being of the individual. Several transitions can be identified as from work life to retirement; from youthful times to the older adult decade (65–74); at the onset of old age (75–84); and during the transition to the frail elderly (85 plus). Those who have experienced these transitions are very likely to be the best resources to help those who are currently experiencing them.

We also remember that health care has components that are regulated by the state. As Christians, we seek to obey civil laws and design programs compatible with those laws. We do well to seek professional counsel when we undertake programs governed by the laws of the state.

Consider the following possibilities for health ministry among older adults.

1. Include older adults as members of a congregational health and wellness committee.
2. Organize Bible study groups to stress the importance of caring for the whole person.
3. Mobilize a family/individual health survey for the congregation.
4. Provide Bible study sessions that deal with stress, loneliness, and related subjects.
5. Sponsor health education activities, health screening events, and exercise programs for members of the congregation and community.
6. Provide health information through a "medical minute" at church activities.
7. Arrange a presentation by a physical therapist to help the elderly to value exercise and to discover ways to compensate for some physical losses.
8. Advertise health topics and events at local hospitals and in the community. Place this information in a monthly community calendar of events for older adults and advertise via posters.
9. Sponsor Red Cross blood drives, perhaps on a Sunday morning.
10. Sponsor educational events on topics like "normal aging" to alleviate myths and fears.
11. Maintain a close relationship with Lutheran agencies and capitalize on their expertise.
12. Research members' professional talents and ask them to develop appropriate health programs.
13. Demonstrate healthful diets by the type of food served at church-sponsored events.
14. Organize appropriate support groups, such as for the bereaved and singles.
15. Consider establishing a parish nurse program. For informa-

tion, contact Concordia University Wisconsin (www.cuw.edu), and the Board for Human Care of The Lutheran Church—Missouri Synod (www.lcms.org).

16. Understand family caregivers' stress and help them to find and use church and community resources.
17. Develop ongoing wellness programs for the whole congregation, including the disabled and homebound.
18. Encourage older adults to package all their medications and have the prescription and non-prescription drugs evaluated by a pharmacist.
19. Understand the needs of people with drug or alcohol dependency. Open your facilities to support groups.
20. Openly discuss all forms of abuse: adult to adult, older adults to each other, children to older adults, etc. Utilize support groups.
21. Encourage a non-smoking policy in church facilities.
22. Be alert to those who are allergic to perfumes, etc. and find solutions to their needs satisfactory to them and others.
23. Create opportunities to learn more about resources for those who are mentally or physically disabled.
24. Encourage older adults to ask for personal assistance when assistance is needed.
25. Inform others about available community programs for personal health and wellness and give encouragement to follow a moderate, reasonable lifestyle of healthy diet, exercise, and regular check-ups.
26. Make sure homes contain no obstacles that can cause older adults to fall or to feel excluded from others in the household.
27. Make available driver's education programs for older persons and programs that teach defensive driving. Encourage older adults to know when "to get out of the driver's seat." Inform them of the availability of public transportation to meet their needs.

28. Enroll in a Red Cross first-aid course, especially to learn CPR and other emergency procedures.
29. Serve as volunteers at a local hospital, hospice unit, or alcohol and drug treatment center.

9 INTERGENERATIONAL MINISTRY

When we talk about intergenerational ministry, or cross-generational ministry, we are discussing the ministry of older adults and younger people to one another and the ministry of older adults and younger people together for the benefit of others. Earlier we noted that today there may be as many as four generations of people in every congregation. As St. Paul teaches, all of the people in these generations together are members of the body of Christ. Each member of the body of Christ is to function with the others, so that entire body can carry out its mission. To the Romans St. Paul wrote, "For as in one body we have many members, and the members do not all have the same function, so we, though many, are one body in Christ, and individually members one of another. Having gifts that differ according to the grace given to us, let us use them: if prophecy, in proportion to our faith" (Romans 12:4–6). In 1 Corinthians, we read similar words: "To each is given the manifestation of the Spirit for the common good" (1 Corinthians 12:7).

The Bible gives examples of intergenerational ministry. As we previously observed, the older Paul and the younger Timothy worked together for the benefit of others during St. Paul's second missionary journey (Acts 16:1–5). When Jesus visited the temple at the age of 12 years, He and the teachers ministered to one another (Luke 2:41–50). With the ever-increasing number of older adults in Christian congregations, we will do well to examine not only how we are ministering to older adults but also how well we are intentionally working to break down unfortunate age divisions that separate members of the body of Christ from one another.

. . . by 2020, when the last Baby Boomer reaches 65, 25 percent of the country's population will be over 65.[3]

Sociologically, churches are intergenerational institutions. They are a group of four or five very different age-divided and separated groups who might not know each other, enjoy each other, or serve each other. However, once in the door on Sundays the believers are truly the one body of Jesus Christ gathered around the Word and Sacraments. This is the strength and beauty of the family of God. Here age differences can and do disappear by the grace God gives us in Word and Sacrament. God's grace in our baptism makes us who we are.

Consider some facts and figures once again. Two-thirds of all persons 65 or older who have ever lived are alive today.[1] The over 65s are growing more than twice as fast as the rest of the population.[2] In fact, by 2020, when the last Baby Boomer reaches 65, 25 percent of the country's population will be over 65.[3] The number will probably be higher in congregations. In the future, will more than a quarter of our members be left just sitting in the pews or at home, isolated and labeled "the oldies," or will they be part of vibrant, intergenerational congregations who embrace and encourage them in ministry with all generations?

Suggestions for intergenerational ministry are offered below with the hope that some may help us move forward to new and exciting intergenerational ministries. These suggestions are listed according to the categories we used above. Some of them have already been noted in different contexts but are repeated here for their intergenerational emphasis. Also, the repetition is to make the ideas readily identifiable and available for the reader without turning back to the earlier pages.

Worship

1. Involve people of all ages in worship services as appropriate.
2. In preparing for worship, enlist intergenerational families to serve on the altar guild; to place hymnals and to stock visitor cards; to usher and to greet; or to create liturgical art and banners for worship services.
3. On confirmation Sunday, recognize the confirmands' extended families and (if known) the person(s) in the congregation with the earliest confirmation date(s).
4. Have confirmands ask a particular older adult to pray for them during their study and invite these prayer partners to be their special guests at the confirmation service.
5. Plan a Senior Sunday. Have youth serve as hosts to older members. Young adults can provide transportation to and from church if needed. Serve a meal afterward.
6. Enlist both older adults and younger persons as volunteers to shepherd a homebound person in worship, in prayer, and as a helpful general resource.
7. Encourage grandparents to invite their grandchildren to be partners with them in worship.
8. Include all appropriate ages in intergenerational prayer chains.
9. Show your welcome of all people, particularly those with disabilities, by providing: an adequate sound system; adequate lighting; the Order of Service printed out (including the hymns); some enlarged on the photocopier; handicapped parking areas; a few hymnals and Bibles with large print; bulletin boards at an appropriate height for those with bifocals or in wheelchairs; and elevators or adequate ramps, if your church or fellowship hall is not accessible to those with mobility problems.

10. If appropriate, offer children's messages suitable for all age levels.

Fellowship

1. Include all ages on the assimilation committee or in other programs designed to assimilate new members into the congregation's life.
2. Encourage intergenerational groups that formulate their own programs.
3. Form new groups frequently as groups become saturated or "closed" after only two or three years. This happens when those in the groups become like family. New groups mean new growth and new opportunities for inclusion. More choices mean more involvement.
4. Encourage older adults to share in the congregation's intergenerational programs. Groups formed around similar interests (golf, camping, fishing, etc.) as well as all-congregation outings to plays, music concerts, sports events, spiritual retreats, and forums discussing major congregational decisions, such as a new building program, should intentionally include opportunities for all members to be together.
5. In a congregation that has a Lutheran Day School, a group of older adults could "adopt" the students from a grade for one year. For example, for one year adopt the second graders. Have treats for them on special occasions, serve as chaperones on outings, etc.
6. Encourage youth and adults to join in preparing programs for the entire congregation, for example, plays and concerts.

Stewardship

1. Encourage older adults' membership with younger people on all congregational boards and committees.
2. If older adults have been serving in positions longer than they desire, consider having them serve as mentors for the

new and younger office holders.

3. Help members plan their retirement years. Start early, and then assist retirees in the God-guided redesigning of their callings with a view to the intergenerational shape of the Christian congregation.
4. Offer opportunities for young and old together to discuss wills, living trusts, living wills, durable power of attorney, and ethical issues such as use of life-support systems, organ donation, and similar subjects.
5. Provide sessions on Medicare, Medicaid, home health services, nursing homes, long-term health insurance, and reverse mortgages on homes. Encourage retirees and their children (and other potential caregivers) to attend.
6. Present specific short-term opportunities for Christian service for young and old in the congregation/District/Synod and community. Retirees have new freedom for travel and visiting family but strongly continue to seek and need service opportunities of a limited duration.
7. Initiate and participate in a mentor program to enable older adults to mentor school-age children in the church and/or the community.
8. Develop a congregational consciousness to care for the environment and preserve resources. Encourage the entire congregation, young and old alike, to use biodegradable materials and to participate in recycling programs.
9. Members of all ages are to encourage and aid one another to be good stewards of their time, treasure, and talents in carrying forward the mission of the church.

Spiritual Care for Fellow Christians

1. Ask older adult volunteers to serve as mentors for a confirmation-class member.
2. An older couple could be asked to be mentors for a newly married couple.

3. Plan issue-oriented Bible studies occasionally so members of different generations may share their varied experiences and insights for mutual learning, understanding, and growth.
4. Invite staff of Lutheran agencies and similar organizations to discuss family life that includes grandparenting, older adults relating to adult children, neglect and abuse, and other pertinent subjects.
5. Invite older adults to share their experiences when a Sunday School or Lutheran Day School class studies historic events they remember.
6. Invite older adults to teach Vacation Bible School and/or Sunday School.
7. Provide topics on retirement, such as attitudes, housing, use of time, financial matters, legal affairs, and other issues, and invite both retired and to-be-retired members to attend.
8. Encourage the young people's group to tape-record or video-record the congregation's oral history, using older members as a resource. Make the materials available through the church library.
9. Set up classes for older adults on the use of computers to be taught by teenagers or young adults.
10. Ask older adult volunteers to teach or promote Bible study classes relating to life crises.

Spiritual Care for Non-Christians

1. Use intergenerational teams when visiting new residents in the community and nursing homes.
2. Encourage older adults to share their faith with young people and testify to them about God's actions in their lives.
3. Use older adults to share their faith with young adults and youth at special times of bereavement, loneliness, and during crisis situations.

4. Encourage all levels to share the Gospel by using their musical, artistic, and dramatic talents.
5. Use older adults to serve as educators in the congregation's outreach program.
6. Involve older adults in visiting guests at worship services.
7. Invite older adults to teach English-as-a-second-language classes.

Physical Care for Christians and Non-Christians

Daily Living Care

1. Recruit persons of all ages to serve on the congregation's human care committee or the service committee.
2. Develop a talent bank as a resource in caring for others.
3. Encourage young adults to assist older adults who need transportation.
4. Encourage older adults to assist children and youth needing transportation for after-school events at church.
5. Take part in a "servant event" and involve all members of the church family.
6. Encourage appropriately-experienced older adults, as well as younger persons, to serve as Laborers for Christ and/or in national programs such as Habitat for Humanity, and to share their experiences with the congregation.
7. Encourage volunteers of all ages to provide a variety of services at nursing homes, hospitals, clinics, etc. For example, parishioners' cars and vans can transport volunteers to a nursing home to serve as "feeders" at the noon meal.
8. Encourage older adults to assist in Day Schools, serve children with special needs, monitor and read aloud to children, serve as "grandparents" in preschools and schools for students whose grandparents are not available.
9. Encourage older adults to volunteer as workers in summer camp programs.

10. Encourage older adults to serve as sponsors for youth activities.
11. Encourage younger adults to deliver tapes, videos, books from the church library, and altar flowers, etc., to the homebound.
12. Enlist people of all ages to provide a food pantry and clothing for the needy.

Health Care

1. Include older adults on the congregation's health and wellness committee.
2. Have the Bible classes include topics on stress, aging, loneliness, wellness, diet, physical therapy, and abuse, including abuse to and by older adults. Invite professionals to speak.
3. Plan an all-congregation seminar addressing programs for parents and children on health-care services by government agencies, Medicare, Medicaid, Social Security insurance, home care, nursing-home insurance, Meals on Wheels, etc.
4. Open facilities of the church to health-related support groups for people of all ages who are dealing with alcohol and drug abuse, grieving, divorce, mental illness, Alzheimer's disease, etc.
5. Create a roster of your congregation's health professionals—doctors, nurses, therapists, health educators, etc., who can be a resource for planning and conducting programs and services.
6. Promote and/or sponsor health and wellness activities at church, such as screenings, informational classes, exercise classes, and support groups.
7. Sponsor Red Cross blood drives.

8. Demonstrate healthful diets by the type of food served at church-sponsored events.
9. Consider initiating a Parish Nurse Program, which has been successful and appreciated in a growing number of congregations.

The time before retirement is a valuable period for ministry to older adults.

10 Ways of Ministering to Special Needs

Pre-Retirement

The years before retirement give individuals opportunity to plan for retirement. Pre-retirement days are times to look to the future and begin the task of redesigning a person's multifaceted calling. Too often people make few or no plans for retirement and find retirement days difficult and boring. They are not sure what to do with themselves and may sometimes feel guilty that they are not continuing what they were doing or doing something fulfilling and useful in the present. They are at loose ends and find retirement far from satisfying. They may become depressed and possibly come to depend on drugs and alcohol to escape their unhappiness and lack of direction. For all of us it is vitally important to use pre-retirement days, relying on the leading of God, to make plans for retirement, to identify what the new aspects of our calling as Christians will be and how we can use the days ahead for the benefit of ourselves and others.

Today many people look forward to retirement as an opportunity to be of service to others in ways not possible in pre-retirement days. Others want to travel and combine pleasure with service. They begin to think more earnestly of the legacy they want to leave when they die. The time before retirement is a valuable period for ministry to older adults. We can alert those about to retire to the importance of discovering and affirming new facets of their Christian calling and encourage them to be mutually supportive and helpful to each other.

Where do we begin? First, at various intervals, we can identify those soon to retire and then invite them to meet together to plan for a satisfying and valuable retirement. We may want to review with them some of the facts and ideas presented in this book, call upon retired persons and retirement counselors to meet with them to give information, encouragement, and motivation, and to prayerfully lead them through a process of planning.

Persons planning retirement at any age may appreciate the opportunity to get to know each other better and the time to come together to share and pray together about their pre-retirement situations. We can facilitate this time. In addition, they may choose to form a new network of friends and fellow retirees by forming social groups and by making plans that include common interests and activities, such as taking cruise trips together or traveling and camping together with their travel trailers or motor homes. They will likely be interested in short-term involvement in activities.

Early Retirement

Today many individuals are retiring earlier than age 65. At the present time in the United States the average age of retiring persons is 57.5 years.[1] These and other early retirees obviously have more time than many retirees to live their lives as they choose and to make valuable contributions to the lives of others.

If early retirees enjoy good health, they likely do not think of themselves as elderly. Like many of today's newly-retired at about age 65, they may prefer not to join in many activities of older retirees. But they may greatly appreciate the opportunity to gather with other early retirees in order to enjoy leisure activities, to work on retirement plans, and to join with them in pursuing opportunities for enriching the lives of others, including the lives of adults older than themselves. We can assist them in meeting with other early retirees and in formulating and carrying out their plans.

Some early retirees may want both to receive and carry out acts of ministry we have previously included in lists that offer suggestions for ministry to and by older adults. Other early retirees are likely to participate eagerly in periodic events, usually short-time opportunities and short-term group activities for both pleasure and helpfulness to others. Remember that many, or most, of them want to focus on being significant and to contribute to the common good.

Boomers' Retirement

In this book we have referred to the large number of people, called Baby Boomers, who will begin to retire in 2011. As we consider how to minister among older adults, it is important for us to give special attention to this massive group of people who will burgeon the number of older adults in the United States in the early decades of the twenty-first century.

Recent studies prepared by the American Association of Retired Persons, reported in 1998 and 2004, provide us with findings about Baby Boomers' expectations for retirement. These studies offer valuable information for ministry among older adults of the Baby Boom era.[2] The AARP studies emphasize the diversity among Baby Boomers. They have different concerns, hopes, dreams, and expectations for retirement.

On the financial front, there will be income disparities between the older (leading age) Boomers and the younger (trailing age) Boomers. Non-retirement income will likely decline between the older and younger Boomers.

The 2004 AARP survey, "Baby Boomers Envision Retirement II," presents its key findings in the following summary statements:

1. Dramatic positive shift [in comparison with the 1998 study] in Boomers' attitudes toward and confidence in Social Security.
2. Boomers are more confident now than five years ago that Medicare will be available when they reach age 65.

3. Boomers remain optimistic about retirement . . .
4. . . . But their expectations, particularly those related to finance, have become much more conservative. (Recent economic conditions and investment scandals have altered Boomers' financial expectations for retirement.)
5. Boomers' primary definitions of retirement, however, are largely unchanged since 1998. (The majority of Boomers view retirement primarily as an opportunity to spend more time with their families, to pursue hobbies and interests, as well as a time for leisure activities.)
6. Most Boomers expect to work in retirement—fewer for fun.
7. Recreation and service continue to factor into Boomers' expectations for retirement.
8. Family should provide for emotional, not financial, support during retirement. (Although Boomers reject the idea of relying on others for financial support during retirement, more Boomers have assumed care-giving responsibilities for their aging parents, and considerable proportions expect to provide financially for parents *and* children during retirement.)
9. Boomers increasingly acknowledge health issues. (Boomers are almost evenly divided between those who are planning for and anticipate having a healthy and active retirement and those who do not.)
10. Many anticipate inadequate health coverage. (About half of Boomers expect to have adequate health insurance . . . many others believe their health coverage in retirement will be lacking.)
11. But growing minorities think they will have health care on their own terms.
12. Boomers are not stuck at "Thirty-Something," but continue to feel younger than they really are. (The mean age among Baby Boomers is 47, but the mean age that [they feel] is 40.)
13. Confidence in ability to prepare for retirement unchanged.

14. Fewer believe personal investments will provide sufficient income for retirement.

15. Boomers are slowly augmenting retirement savings portfolios.

16. Polarization of the retirement expectations of Have and Have-nots continues. (Differences among the [rich and poor] with regard to income, optimism about retirement, and preparedness continue to be evident.)

17. 1998 Boomer segmentation still holds true today, as does the view that a "one-size-fits-all" retirement solution is unworkable for Boomers. ([T]he five well-defined groups of Baby Boomers—the Strugglers, the Anxious, the Self-Reliant, the Enthusiasts, and the Traditionalists.)

18. Many of those who were merely Anxious before are now Strugglers in today's weak economy.

19. The outlook of Traditionalists has dimmed. ([M]any more now feel that they will need to work during retirement for the income it provides.)[3]

Those who write about Boomers offer a variety of opinions. Some identify two classes of Boomers. They speak of the older Boomers, born between 1946 and 1954, as Leading-Edge Boomers, and the younger Boomers, born between 1955 and 1964, as Trailing-Edge Boomers. The Leading-Edge Boomers number 34,000,000 persons and the Trailing-Edge total 42,000,000.

Baby Boomers are much more concerned with aging well than they are with aging in general

About the Leading-Edge Boomers, writers comment that because of their place in American history and culture, the older Boomers have fared better than younger Boomers. They were the first to go to college, to obtain jobs, and to buy houses. Older Boomers acquired better jobs, better opportunities for career advancement, and better house prices. While older Boomers grew up in stable homes, younger Boomers grew up in less stable families in an era of rising divorce rates in America. Leading-Edge Boomers are generally more financially secure than Trailing-Edge Boomers.[4]

Some investigators of Boomers as a group offer us a number of observations related to our ministry interests. I note the following as pertinent:

1. Boomers will view old age as not starting until 80. They will consider people in their 60s and 70s as middle-aged. At retirement they will insist that their lives are only half over.[5]

2. Boomers will look upon retirement as "more of a mid-life event, when their nests turn blissfully empty, years of routine work is behind them, and their paid-off consumer debt has enabled them to become investors. They look at the prospects of traveling, beginning new (but less-demanding) careers, starting up interesting new businesses, and having time do all those things they never had time (or money) to do as they car-pooled, van-pooled, funded college savings plans, and watched as their kids flew the coop."[6]

3. "Baby Boomers are much more concerned with aging well than they are with aging in general, thus their emphasis on staying active, becoming more educated, and keeping themselves at the cutting edge at what they consider to be mid-life."[7]

4. Boomers, according to one observer, "are going to figure out this thing called aging like no other generation ever has. It's my guess that what they love to do now they will continue to do in slightly different versions well into their 80s and 90s. It is possible as the Baby Boomers age there will be a whole shift from a youth-oriented culture to a 'maturity movement.' The second half of life will most likely include the pursuit of meaning and an attitude of how can I help society with 'what I've learned in life.' Boomers will continue to want to contribute—and that's good!"[8]

5. Church participation among Boomers, particularly the older ones, is on the rise. About 42 percent of Leading-Edge Boomers are church-involved. Those who go back to church look for religious education for their children and

> seek some kind of religious experience that enables them to make sense of their lives.[9]

What we learn about Boomers when they retire indicates that much of what we say in this book applies to them as to all older adults. However, our studies suggest that we need to recognize that when Boomers retire, they are likely to be and see themselves as younger and more vigorous than the majority of older adults before them and have many pursuits in mind for retirement. Many will be attracted to planning and participating in activities that enable them both to enjoy life and contribute to the good of others. They will be interested in short-term educational and servant events. Boomers will enjoy recreational and travel opportunities. Our task is to facilitate that planning and support their chosen activities.

We assist Boomers in choosing and pursuing their goals by helping them to use their time before retirement to plan and test out what they choose to do. By doing things together before they retire, they will both think ahead and achieve a sense of community among themselves that will continue in retirement. This calls us to be innovative in involving Boomers in Christian service as retirement approaches and before it begins.

The following ideas both summarize and expand elements for reaching Boomers that we have considered. Adapted from an article in *CASA Energizing Seniors*, "Boomers and Ministry" by Bruce Edwards, the following are ideas for engaging Boomers today, as well as in the future when they retire.

1. Ministries (Christian service activities) that contain the components of meaning and purpose will engage Boomers. These might include short-term evangelism endeavors and activities that will make an impression upon the community. Boomers will invest their time and resources in activities they consider to have meaning and purpose.

2. For Boomers to feel a sense of belonging in their acts of Christian service, they need to participate in the direction and planning of what they do. They desire ownership in their ministry.

3. Boomer women desire active roles in planning and pursuing the Christian service activities in which they participate.

4. Service opportunities need to be designed to enable people to come, serve, and at the same time be able to enjoy their retirement years.
5. When it is in keeping with Scriptural principles, congregations need to make use of community resources in their Christian service. Such inclusion benefits the community and the congregation that has limited resources.
6. Encourage and enable Boomers to develop and pursue service opportunities based on their life experiences.[10]

Several Internet sites give information about Boomers that you may find helpful in shaping ministry among Boomers before and after they retire. Among them are the Boomer Café (www.boomercafe.com),
My Prime Time (www.myprimetime.com),
ThirdAge (www.thirdage.com),
Baby Boomer Headquarters (www.bbhq.com),
Boomernet (www.boomernet.com),
and Boomers International (http://boomersint.org/home.htm).

Young Older Adults

Many retirees today do not think of themselves as old. Just as Boomers will likely regard themselves when they retire, today's retirees think of themselves as still young or younger than other older adults. They will not want to join older adult groups and do things that many older adults ordinarily enjoy doing. Rather, they have many of the interests we have ascribed above to those who retire early and to Boomers when they retire. They will be interested in short-term educational and servant events and will enjoy recreational and travel opportunities.

As we minister among older adults, we will do our job well if we recognize the diversity among older adults. We are challenged with the responsibility of seeing them as they see themselves. We will help them explore their needs and wants and support them in addressing their needs in unique and creative ways.

Losses

Older adults experience a variety of painful losses. Among their losses are the loss of a job, an accustomed pattern of daily living, health, the family home, financial resources, and the death of a spouse or other relatives and close friends. Some are deeply saddened by the death of a cherished pet. These losses often generate guilty feelings about things wrongly done or said and things left undone and unsaid.

With losses we experience grief that can be destructive to our lives if we don't deal with it in positive ways. Older adults, like all of us, need people to be close to them who will help them with their grief work. They need what we all require when we are grieving. We need caring people to listen to us patiently and empathically as we talk about our difficult experiences. We need people to stay close to us, give us hope, and help us restructure our lives.

To be more specific, those who grieve have need of people who are close to them to help them accept their loss and pain as real, to review the lost relationship, to accept and work through their feelings, to express their sorrow, to affirm their hope, and to develop new relationships and a new lifestyle. The pastor and those who serve older adults do grief work by listening caringly, supportively, and prayerfully; by giving information about the grief experience; by speaking the Gospel of hope and forgiveness; by fostering old and new relationships; and by assisting with plans for the future. Those who minister to older adults will do well to initiate support groups for grieving persons or encourage them to participate in appropriate groups already formed. People acquainted with like experiences are capable of being extremely helpful to those who grieve.

For older adults whose loved ones have died in the Lord, the assurances of Holy Baptism offer great comfort and hope. Baptized into the death and resurrection of Jesus Christ, their loved ones received the gifts of new and eternal life in Christ. In his letter to the Romans St. Paul wrote:

> Do you not know that all of us who have been baptized into Christ Jesus were baptized into His death? We were buried therefore with Him by baptism into death, in order that, just as Christ was raised from the dead by the glory of the Father, we too might walk in newness of life. For if we have been united with

> Him in a death like His, we shall certainly be united with Him in a resurrection like His. (Romans 6:3–5)

In Baptism our Christian loved ones were incorporated into the body of Christ, and in death they have gone from the church on earth to the church victorious in heaven.

In our grief we recognize as Christians our closeness and fellowship with our loved ones who die in the Lord; this closeness is very real for us. Because we are united with Christ through faith, those who have departed this life in the sign of faith are close to us, and we are close to them. Words of a hymn speak of our faith: "The saints on earth and those above But one communion make; Joined to their Lord in bonds of love, All of His grace partake. One family, we dwell in Him, One Church above, beneath; Though now divided by the stream, The narrow stream, of death."[11]

Fellowship with all of God's people on earth and in heaven flows from our baptismal identity and becomes very real for us in our celebrations of the Holy Communion. In these celebrations we share together in the body and blood of Jesus and, at the same time, remember that this Supper is also a foreshadowing and foretaste of the heavenly feast that departed people of God already enjoy. We both share in a salvation feast that God has prepared.

In the Holy Communion liturgy we share in the fellowship of those in heaven as we join them in singing the hymn that angels sang at the birth of Jesus and still sing today: "Glory be to God on high" or "Glory to God in the highest." Then, just before receiving our Lord's body and blood in the Sacred Meal, we join in a song with angels, archangels, and all the company of heaven that truly includes our departed loved ones. We joyfully hear, "Therefore with angels and archangels and with all the company of heaven we laud and magnify your glorious name, evermore praising you and saying: 'Holy, holy, holy Lord, God of Sabaoth [hosts]. Heav'n and earth are full of your glory. Hosanna, hosanna, hosanna in the highest.'"[12]

We are bold to claim our closeness in the celebration of the Holy Communion with those who have gone before us in the sign of faith because Holy Scripture affirms what we have said. After He had instituted the Lord's Supper Jesus said to His disciples, "I tell you I will not drink again of this fruit of the vine until that day when I drink it new with you in my Father's kingdom" (Matthew 26:29). In the book of Revelation St. John records that he "heard what seemed to be the loud voice of a great multitude in heaven, crying out, 'Hallelujah! Salvation and glory and power belong to our God, for His judgments are true and just' " (Revelation 19:1–2). Then, St. John "heard what seemed to be the voice of a great multitude, like the roar of many waters and like the sound of mighty peals of thunder, crying out, 'Hallelujah! For the Lord our God the Almighty reigns. Let us rejoice and exult and give him the glory!' " (Revelation 19:6–7). Thanks to God His people on earth and in heaven join to praise Him, for they are of one fellowship.

In ministering to those whose Christian loved ones have gone before us, we happily help them to understand this blessed fellowship and encourage them to think of it and rejoice in it as they receive the body and blood of Jesus Christ in the meal He has given us for forgiveness of sins, life, and salvation. As we share his banquet on earth, so with our loved ones we shall soon share in the festal banquet in heaven. We are close to Jesus and to all His perfected saints. How good He is to keep us close to Him and to the saints beyond!

Impending Death

Older persons, perhaps more than those who are younger, think about their impending death. Because of their age, death appears closer than in years past. We minister to them by giving them the opportunity to talk with us, and to talk with one another, about their impending death and by reviewing with them the promises God has made to His baptized people about life in the world to come. St. Paul comforts us with the words: "For I am sure that neither death nor life, nor angels nor rulers, nor things present nor things to come, nor powers, nor height nor depth, nor anything else in all creation, will be able to separate us from the love of God in Christ Jesus our Lord" (Romans 8:38–39). Nothing, not even death, can separate us from God and His protective love.

There may be older persons, like many others of all ages, who do not think about the reality of impending death and do not consciously prepare for death. We serve them well if we help them to confront the reality of death and affirm God's promises of eternal life that were given by God

Nothing, not even death, can separate us from God and His protective love.

in Holy Baptism. St. Paul gives us this assurance to share with one another: "He [God] saved us, not because of works done by us in righteousness, but according to His own mercy, by the washing of regeneration and renewal of the Holy Spirit, whom He poured out on us richly through Jesus Christ our Savior, so that being justified by His grace we might become heirs according to the hope of eternal life" (Titus 3:4–7). St. Peter adds his words of certainty, "Blessed be the God and Father of our Lord Jesus Christ! According to His great mercy, He has caused us to be born again to a living hope through the resurrection of Jesus Christ from the dead, to an inheritance that is imperishable, undefiled, and unfading, kept in heaven for you, who by God's power are being guarded through faith for a salvation ready to be revealed in the last time" (1 Peter 1:3–5). Paul expressed the Christian conviction of all of us when he said, "For to me to live is Christ, and to die is gain" (Philippians 1:21). Paul said of himself as a Christian, "My desire is to depart and be with Christ" (Philippians 1:23).

What else might we do for older adults who prepare for death? Among our acts of service we might beneficially encourage them to consider arranging for power of attorney, organ donation, and living will documents. Older adults may need encouragement and assistance to make plans for their funeral service and burial and to prepare wills and trusts for the distribution of their possessions at the time of death. Many will be grateful if we put them in touch with a competent attorney or estate planner to attend to their legal needs.

Depression

Of all Americans 65 and older, an estimated 2 million have depressive illness. Another 5 million may have depressive symptoms.[13] Depression in older adults seems to increase the risk for death by illness and by suicide. Persons 65 and older account for 18 percent of all suicides in the United States in 2000.[14]

Certain risk factors for depression in older adults have been identified. Among them are the following: some medicines or combination of medicines, illness, changes in the function of the brain, social isolation, recent loss and bereavement, chronic pain, loss of body strength and parts, fear of death, past suicide attempts, drug abuse, and family history of depression. Health workers encourage those who care for older adults to watch for depression and do things for them that will help them toward recovery. This is very important because only 10 percent of older depressed persons seek help.[15] Often they do not seek help because they feel ashamed or hopeless.

Hope and help are available for older adults who suffer from depression. Physicians have treatment to offer. As Christians we are able to reassure depressed persons that they are not "crazy" but are experiencing a condition that many experience. When they feel unloved, we are able to assure them of God's love and demonstrate our love and concern for them by our actions. We can stand by them and encourage them to talk about what is going on in their lives and assist them in possibly discovering depression-causing factors in their lives. We give help by our own acts of care and by putting depressed persons in touch with professionals and others who can be caring, supportive, helping, and healing persons in their lives.

Addictions

Three addictions often associated with older adults are addictions to drugs (both licit and illicit), alcohol, and gambling. This means that a significant number of older adults lose control over their use of drugs, alcohol, and gambling activities. All these addictions endanger and adversely affect their lives and the lives of those close to them.

Drug addiction in older adults is frequently initiated by lengthy use and abuse of prescribed and over-the-counter drugs. Some begin to use illicit drugs in their older years and lose their control over them; others take their drug addictions with them into their older years. Aging makes older adults more susceptible to the effects of the drugs they ingest.

Gambling often becomes a pastime for older adults that grows into an addiction. One report states that in 1997, the casinos in Atlantic City earned $3.8 billion, with 65 percent of that money coming from patrons over the age of 55.[16] Addiction to gambling has dire results in the lives of older adults as well as in the lives of younger persons, sometimes with more critical results. Older adults can readily gamble away their limited retirement income and savings, and they are without the long-term ability to regain what they have lost.

As it sometimes is with abusers of other drugs, many alcoholics bring their addictions with them into their later years. Others become addicted rather rapidly when they begin drinking or as their drinking intensifies. For some, drinking triggers a proclivity for alcohol addiction. Many older adults drink more and more and lose their control over alcohol because they are bored or depressed and/or socialize with persons who are heavy drinkers. No matter the reasons for inappropriate drinking, the abuse of alcohol is destructive in their lives, increasingly causing spiritual, physical, mental, financial, social, and legal problems. At any rate, health officials call substance abuse an "invisible epidemic" that affects 17 percent of America's older adults.[17]

The tragedy of addictions is that addicted persons do not recognize their loss of control; they deny their adverse behavior and rationalize their addictive lifestyle. Only when the pain of addictive behavior becomes greater than the pleasure people derive from their addictions are they open to help.

What can we do? It behooves us to "speak the truth in love" to them again and again. We give them the facts about addictions, how their addiction is hurting them and others, and what they can do to recover. Most important, we must be careful not to enable and facilitate their addictive behavior.

There are many recovery programs for addicted people, many are mutual-help Twelve Step Program groups that can be given Christian meaning by Christian participants. I talk about this extensively in my books *The Twelve Steps*, *When Addictions Threaten*, and *Freedom from Hurtful Behaviors*. I recommend these helpful books to you, available from Concordia Publishing House.

Those who are emotionally close to addicted persons are hurtfully and painfully affected by their abuses. They, too, need support, direction, and help. There are also support groups for their recovery. Addiction is very much a family problem.

For addicted persons the pain of their drinking is God telling them that they are living disobedient and destructive lives. When, in the depths of their pain, they hear the indictment of God in His Word and His word of love and forgiveness in Jesus Christ and turn to Him for help, God responds with the greatest of help. He gladly and readily proclaims to them His love and His offer of forgiveness and power for renewal of life gained for all of us by His Son Jesus. When, by the power of God working through the Gospel, they turn to God in faith, God richly endows them with all His spiritual gifts and blessings. On our part, we are to be the voice of God in their lives so God's voice is known and heard and enabled to work vigorously.

As members of Christ's Church we have opportunity to provide Christian support groups for addicted people as well as for others with a variety of needs. In addition, we can give a meeting place in our parish buildings to community support groups that seek to help others.

Hurting and Fearful Older Adults

Some older people knowing that death is not far ahead begin to feel that they have accomplished little in their lives. It is often helpful to give them opportunity to review their life's journey in detail and assist them in identifying their contributions. When they recognize their failures, we are ready to speak God's Gospel of forgiveness into their ears and hearts. When they identify their successes, it is good for us to thank God with them for the many ways in which they have enriched the lives of others.

There are older adults who have been rejected and abandoned by one, some, or all of their children. They may have been the subjects of physical and emotional abuse. How can we help? Again, we help by listening to their stories and by taking appropriate actions and doing interventions that might lessen or alleviate their pain and bring about positive changes in relationships. If changes cannot be effected, we need to intensify our closeness and care for hurting persons. Assure them that God gives us strength to accept and grow from painful experiences and then lead them along the path of acceptance and growth.

When older persons have spiritual, physical, mental, social, medical, financial, and legal needs, we can do much to put them in touch with resources that are available in the community and in the church. All too often older persons do not know where to turn for assistance with pressing needs or they are hesitant to ask for aid. We can help.

Alzheimer's Disease

Estimates suggest that Alzheimer's disease currently afflicts 4.2 to 5.8 million Americans. Projections indicate that the number of Americans with Alzheimer's could more than triple to 16 million Americans by the middle of the century.

Alzheimer's disease afflicts an estimated one in 10 persons over age 65 and almost half of those 85 and older. The disease is the most common cause of intellectual dysfunction among people aged 65 and older. It lasts from two to 20 years, and patients live on an average of eight to 10 years from the time of diagnosis. There is yet no cure for the disease; however, there are new drugs that relieve symptoms and retard the progression of the illness. Researchers hope for preventive and curative medications in the near future.

The Alzheimer's Foundation of America describes the symptoms of the Alzheimer's illness as a progressive, degenerative disease that attacks the brain's nerve cells and results in the loss of memory, thinking, language skills, and behavioral changes. Other symptoms are as follows:

- Alzheimer's disease advances by stages, from early mild forgetfulness to severe dementia.
- During the earliest or mild stage of the disease, classic markers include impaired memory, such as trouble remembering names, faulty judgment, and mood swings.
- Patients typically lose communication skills, forget how to do everyday tasks like bathing and dressing, become suspicious, and suffer delusions when they progress into the middle or moderate stage.
- Severe dementia marks the late or severe stage. Individuals lose all reasoning and language abilities and ambulatory functions, and are unable to swallow.[18]

Persons with Alzheimer's disease obviously need the care of people within and outside their families. As such care is so demanding of time and energy, caregivers also need the help of others. Caregivers need care-giving. Such need points the way for Christian service by both young and old.

Education about Alzheimer's is a significant service we can and should offer with regard to the disease. Both older and younger people need to understand the nature and progression of the illness and the treatment available. Many knowledgeable people, among them medical professionals, are willing to take part in such an educational pursuit.

caregivers also need the help of others

Spouses of Retirees

The spouses of retired persons confront changes in lifestyle when the working spouse retires. Retirement brings a new experience of relationships, schedules, and activities for the entire family, especially for a nonworking, or even still working, spouse. The divorce rate climbs immediately after retirement just as it does in the first five years of marriage.

Spouses may find some new ideas about family life in retirement by getting to know other retired spouses. They have opportunity to discuss together ideas and insights about life in the family after full-time work comes to an end for one or both spouses. A discussion and support group may be just the thing needed. The forming of such a group is worthy of consideration.

Marriage and Remarriage

There are 14.5 million people in the United States 65 and older who are single or single again. The single again are persons whose spouse has died or who are divorced. Those who are single are those who have never married. Among the 14.5 million, both single and single again persons 65 or older get married.[19]

Marriage is a big step for any person, but perhaps even more complex for older adults than for younger persons. As in the case of anyone thinking about getting married, religious affiliation and commitment are important matters to consider. It is also necessary for older persons considering marriage to think and talk about legal, financial, and property issues, familial relationships, and similarities and dissimilarities in general.

Those older divorced persons who are thinking about remarriage have a special responsibility to see to it that their divorce has been properly dealt with in their relationship with God and the Church, as well as in terms of personal issues and interpersonal relationships.

Single persons who would like to marry need to deal with these same concerns. In addition, they will find it wise to think long and hard about what it will be like for them to be married if they have lived alone for many years. This is a must because older single persons have well-defined lifestyles they may find difficult to alter.

As persons who serve among older adults, we need to take opportunity to refer those older adults considering marriage to the pastor and ourselves assist them, as appropriate, in making God-pleasing decisions that will positively influence their marriage or re-marriage plans. Those who are relationally and emotionally close to such persons will have an advantage in carrying out this Christian service.

Living Together Outside of Marriage

A population survey of the Census Bureau shows that about 203,000 households in the United States contain just two unrelated adults, a man and a woman.[20] The nature of the individual relationships is not clear. But we do know that today older adult men and women who are not married are living together. Reasons given for living together outside of marriage often have to do with personal finances and financial matters that may impact each person's family members and relationships.

With regard to government benefits, married persons or couples who are disabled receive a lower rate of Supplemental Security Income (SSI) than unmarried disabled individuals. However, when a spouse remarries after the age of 60, that person is eligible to receive the higher of the Social Security benefits of the former or current spouse. Also, if the benefit a person received as a worker is higher than the spousal benefit, he or she will receive the benefit based on his or her own work record.[21]

There may be certain financial programs, as well as SSI, that penalize individuals who remarry. Even so, such possibilities do not offer a legitimate reason for unmarried individuals to live together as husband and wife. God's Word declares that they are guilty of adultery before Him. Also, they provide a bad example for others, especially young people, and run the risk of offending others. Therefore, Christian persons will not live as husband and wife apart from marriage. Those who do are called to repent—to recognize and confess their disobedience and turn to God with faith in Jesus Christ as their Savior. Surely, God will forgive them for their disobedience and endow them with the power of the Holy Spirit to bring their lives into conformity with God's Law. According to His Word and promise, God will adequately provide for them. This is the promise of Jesus: "But seek first the kingdom of God and His righteousness, and all these things [temporal things such as food and clothing] will be added to you" (Matthew 6:33).

Those of us who serve among older adults are to admonish those who are living in adultery and call them to repentance for forgiveness and newness of life through faith in Jesus. We, who are laypersons, are to refer them to the pastor for his care and then support the counsel he gives.

marriage is the commitment of a man and woman to live together as one for the good of one another

Just as many older men and women say they live together outside of marriage for financial reasons, so many claim they are together only for the purposes of friendship, companionship, and mutual helpfulness. They suggest that their living arrangement is acceptable because they are not sexually active in their relationship.

This position overlooks the fact that the oneness of marriage is more than a sexual relationship. While marriage is the God-ordained relationship for sexual activity between a man and woman, this does not mean that the lack of sexual activity between a man and woman living together nullifies marriage or makes it unnecessary. Marriage is not simply about sex; marriage is more than sex. It is the commitment of a man and woman to live together as one for the good of one another. Many married couples do not have a sexual relationship because of disability, lack of desire, or advanced age. Yet they are grateful to be husband and wife according to God's plan for them.

When a man and woman live together outside of marriage for whatever reasons they may give, they are disobedient to God's will for their lives and need to take corrective action.

Disobedience to God's will is not the only factor to be considered in the relationship of a man and woman living outside of marriage. Such an arrangement offends some people and certainly provides a bad example for other men and women, both young and old. They may readily conclude that marriage is not at all necessary for the relationship of a man and woman living together. Grandchildren may be heard saying, "If Grandma and Jim can live together without being married, why can't John and I do the same thing?" Certainly, young people do not need that kind of modeling in our day and age when many hold marriage in low esteem.

For the Church, older adults struggling with finances and who need companionship and help for everyday living provide a wonderful opportunity for Christian service. Older adults certainly need the care of fellow-Christians in making a God-pleasing choice about marriage when they face the decision about living arrangements. In turn, we are to be helpful to those who marry by providing them with our personal, loving care. We remember that God works through us in the lives of others. We are the means through which God will provide them with daily bread and all that they need for the support of this life.

11 Suggestions for Implementing Ministry among Older Adults in the Christian Congregation

On the basis of what we have discussed in earlier chapters, we are now ready to think about how to intentionally enhance service among older adults in the Christian congregation. First of all, we must affirm that the ministry of which we speak is a congregational ministry, not just the service of a few persons working independently. Ministry among older adults calls for congregational action and participation on many levels.

With whom will the service begin? That depends on who is reading this book and is concerned about ministry among older adults. You may be a pastor, other church professional, congregation member or leader, an older adult, or group of persons interested in ministry among older adults. Whoever you may be, God can begin the ministry with you.

How shall we go about initiating an enhanced program of ministry among older adults? I suggest two possible procedures: a Two-Meeting Model and a Five-Meeting Model. Feel free to adopt or adapt the models. You may choose to design your own format, possibly using components of the procedures I suggest, and design three or four study-planning sessions rather than two or five. For example, you might choose three sessions by doing the "Preparation for the First Meeting" of the Two-Meeting Model at the first of three meetings.

Two-Meeting Model

(Additional ideas and explanations for the two meetings may be gained by reading the Five-Meeting suggestions.)

The Decision to Study Older Adult Ministry

- If you are not the pastor, but a part-time or full-time church worker or an interested member or group of members, contact the pastor and present your interest in the enhancement of the congregation's ministry among older adults.
- With the pastor's approval and support, request the chief administrative body of the congregation (Voters Assembly, Church Council, Board of Directors) to authorize a study and planning group (committee, task force, focus group, team) that includes older adults. This group, with the approval of the pastor, will present its findings and recommendations to the chief administrative body for consideration and implementation.

The Study-Planning Group

- The size of the group and scope of the work to be accomplished can be determined by those who authorize the planning or by the initiator(s) of the group. Older adults and committed leaders, such as past and present officers of the congregation and its organizations, should be considered for membership. The inclusion of older adults is vital.
- The initiator or initiators of the program shall select the members of the study-planning group.

- A final report with recommendations is to be submitted to the congregation's chief administrative body.

Suggested Agendas for Committee Meetings

The way of action proposed now may be accomplished in two meetings. As already suggested, follow or amend these suggestions in ways appropriate for your congregation.

Preparation for the First Meeting

- Make assignments before the first meeting.
- Ask all members of the group to read this book as an orientation to the task. This reading will put the members on common ground for their undertaking.
- Ask members of the group individually or in teams of two or more to:

  Develop congregational profiles using the materials and examples provided in Appendix A. Congregational profiles are an important tool for determining some current and future trends in the congregation. There are examples of completed forms and forms to be completed for a "Total Membership Profile" and for a profile of "Communicant Members 60 Years of Age and Older."

  Create the older adults survey using the forms provided in Appendix A. These surveys ("Survey for Older Adults Ministries" and "Older Adults Inquiry Form"), when they are completed, show the congregation how it is already serving older adults in both the congregation and community and what it can do to enhance existing efforts. Revise the survey instruments to meet your congregation's situation.

  Assemble a list of community resources for older adults.

  Contact community agencies to discover services and opportunities for service available to older adults. You will experience firsthand the difficulty or ease of finding the resources. Bring some of their brochures to the committee meeting.

The First Meeting

- Begin with an opening devotion.
- Give committee members the opportunity to discuss their reading of this book.
- Study and discuss the older adult profiles and older adult surveys.
- Reflect on the list of community resources for older adults.
- Assignments:

  Ask members of the group to review suggested ways of ministry for one function of the church (at least one member for each function) and come to the next meeting with six recommended ways of ministry for the implementation of the function assigned. For this task, encourage the participants also to consider chapters 9 and 10. The relevant "Form For Ministry Comments and Suggestions" (provided in Appendix A) may be helpful in fulfilling this assignment.
- Set the time for the next meeting and close with a prayer.

Second Meeting

- Begin with an opening devotion.
- List for each function of the church, one function at a time (e.g., worship, fellowship, or stewardship), the six suggestions for implementation provided by the committee member or members responsible for the particular function being considered. Then have all members of the committee prioritize the six recommendations. Each person is to participate in the prioritizing process by giving three points to their first choice, two points to their second choice, and one point to their third choice. The three items with the highest total score will have the highest priority and the three items with the lowest total scores will have the lowest priority and can be eliminated. If advisable, the process can be repeated. On the basis of this prioritizing process all the committee members will be able to decide on three activities they wish initially to recommend for the particular

function of the church being considered. This process will produce a comprehensive list of recommendations for implementation that embraces all functions of the church.

- Designate members to prepare a report with committee recommendations for the congregation's chief administrative body and select the person or persons who will present the report.

Implementation

If the chief administrative body accepts the report, that body may ask a member of the committee or the entire study-planning group to become the implementing person or group or make arrangements for the creation of such a group. The implementing person(s) will be responsible for carrying forward the enhancement of the congregation's ministry among older adults under the supervision of the pastor and with accountability to the chief administrative body.

Five-Meeting Model

The Decision to Study Older Adult Ministry

- If you are not the pastor, but a part-time or full-time church worker or an interested member or group of members, contact the pastor and present your interest in the enhancement of the congregation's ministry among older adults.
- With the pastor's approval and support, request the chief administrative body of the congregation (Voters Assembly, Church Council, Board of Directors) to authorize a study-planning committee (task force, focus group, team). This is to be a working committee that will present its findings and recommendations to the chief administrative body for consideration and implementation. Instead of a committee, some congregations might consider a volunteer who is willing to direct and coordinate this first phase and form a committee.

The Committee

- The size of the committee and scope of the work to be accomplished can be determined by those who authorize the study.
- If you are able to have input, you might suggest a committee of six to 10 people. Older adults and committed leaders, such as past and present officers of the congregation and its organizations, should be considered. The use of retirees is vital.
- You will probably need at least five 90-minute meetings.
- Potential committee members should be made aware of the fact that this will be a working committee.
- A final report with recommendations is to be submitted to the chief administrative body of the congregation.

Implementation

- The course of action will be determined by the administrative body.
- It may be necessary for the study committee to monitor the progress of its recommendations.
- The plan is to intentionally enhance ministry among the older adults of the congregation. Encourage the congregation to adopt the best ways to develop this aspect of ministry over a period of time.

Suggested Agendas for Committee Meetings

THE FIRST MEETING

- Begin with an opening devotion.
- Choose a chairperson and secretary for the committee if such leaders have not been designated by the administrative body.
- Review the responsibility of the committee. Its purpose is to assist the congregation in discovering ways (or more

ways) to implement ministry among older adults.

- Assignments:

  Assign chapters 1 through 6 of this book to be read for discussion at the next meeting.

  Designate members to:

  1. Develop congregational profiles using the materials and examples provided in Appendix A. Congregational profiles are an important tool for determining some current and future trends in the congregation. They should also help determine where the greatest program emphasis should be. Keeping up with changes in membership is often difficult. Therefore, it may be difficult to gather needed information. On the other hand, because many congregations have computers and have spent many hours gathering pertinent information about the membership, the data may be readily available. If the congregation has completed profiles in the past five years, this information is useful. See Appendix A for samples of membership profiles and forms to be completed. There are examples of completed forms and forms to be completed for a "Total Membership Profile" and for a profile of "Communicant Members 60 Years of Age and Older."

  2. Create the older adult survey using the form provided in Appendix A. This survey, when it is completed, shows the congregation how it is already serving older adults in both the congregation and community and what it needs to do to enhance existing efforts. Revise the survey instrument to meet your congregation's situation.

  3. In addition to doing this survey, perhaps in preparation for completing it, you might choose to visit older members of the congregation to assist them in completing a personal questionnaire. A form for this pursuit is also found in Appendix A.

  4. Assemble a list of community resources for older adults. Contact community agencies to discover the services and opportunities for service available to older adults. You will

experience firsthand the difficulty or ease of finding the resources. Bring some of their brochures to the committee meeting. Suggested community resources are: The Area Agency on Aging, United Way information and referral services, service agencies, telephone directory, and Internet sites such as those noted in Appendix B.

- Set a date for the next meeting and close with prayer.

THE SECOND MEETING

- Begin with an opening devotion.
- Review the chapters of this book assigned for reading and discussion at this meeting.
- Study and discuss the congregational profiles.
- Review and discuss the older adult profiles and older adult surveys.
- Reflect on the list of community resources for older adults.
- Assignments:

  Read chapters 7 through 11 of this book for review and discussion at the next meeting.

  Have each member review the suggested ways of ministry among older adults related to worship (both congregational and homebound), fellowship, and stewardship. Include in your review suggestions discovered in chapters 9 and 10. Feel free to add to the suggested ways, then choose three ways you would like to implement in your congregation for the areas of congregational worship, homebound worship, fellowship, and stewardship. In carrying out this assignment, it will be helpful for you to note ways the congregation is already ministering to older adults in these areas. You are encouraged to use the forms ("Form for Ministry Comments and Suggestions") provided in Appendix A for doing the assignment.

- Set the date for the next meeting and close with prayer.

THE THIRD MEETING

- Begin with an opening devotion.
- Review the chapters of this book assigned for reading and discussion at this meeting. Give special attention to identifying the functions of the church.

  Step A: For each function being considered, list the three suggestions for implementation provided by each committee member. Have the leader write them on newsprint or a chalkboard. Complete sentences are not necessary.

  Step B: Combine suggestions that are similar.

  Step C: Considering the complete list of suggestions, each person is to participate in the prioritizing process by giving three points for their first choice, two points to their second choice, and one point to their third choice. Then prioritize the first, second, and third choices of each group until three are identified as the top first, second, and third choices of the group.

  Step D: On the basis of the prioritizing process, all the committee members together will be able to decide on three activities they wish to recommend initially for each function of the church. Ultimately, this process will produce a comprehensive list of recommendations for implementation that embraces all functions of the church.
- Report on the worship (congregational and homebound), fellowship, and stewardship assignments by listing and prioritizing the recommendations of the committee members.
- Assignments:

  Read chapter 12 and the conclusion of this book for review and discussion at the next meeting.

  Review the suggested ways of ministry among older adults related to spiritual care for fellow Christians and spiritual care for non-Christians. Include in your review suggestions discovered in chapters 9 and 10. Feel free to add to the suggested ways, then choose three activities for each function that you would like to implement in your congregation.

In carrying out this assignment, it will be helpful for you to note ways the congregation is already ministering to older adults in the areas of spiritual care for Christians and non-Christians. You are encouraged to use the forms ("Form for Ministry Comments and Suggestions") provided in Appendix A for doing the assignment.

- Set the date for the next meeting and close with prayer.

THE FOURTH MEETING

- Begin with an opening devotion.
- Review the sections of this book assigned for reading and discussion at this meeting.
- Report on the spiritual care assignments individually by listing and prioritizing individual recommendations.
- Assignments:

  Review the suggested ways of ministry among older adults related to daily living care for fellow Christians and non-Christians individually and health care for fellow Christians and non-Christians individually. Include in your review suggestions found in chapters 9 and 10. Feel free to add to the suggested ways, then choose three activities for each function that you would like to implement in your congregation. In carrying out this assignment, it will be helpful for you to note ways the congregation is already ministering to older adults in the area of physical care. You are encouraged to use the forms ("Form for Ministry Comments and Suggestions") provided in Appendix A for doing the assignment.

- Set the date for the next meeting and close with prayer.

THE FIFTH MEETING

- Begin with an opening devotion.
- Report on the daily living and health care assignments by listing and prioritizing recommendations for each topic separately.
- Make arrangements for a report with recommendations to be presented to the congregation's primary administrative

body. Such a report should at least include: (1) the names of the study committee; (2) a review of the functions of the church; (3) the congregational profiles and surveys; (4) the list of community resources; (5) the prioritized recommendations; and (6) suggestions for implementation. Several members of the committee should prepare the report. This report, with prioritized recommendations, should then be submitted to the administrative body for implementation. (The proposed process should be done again from time to time to further enhance the congregation's older adult ministry.)

- Close with prayer.

Suggestions for Implementation by the Administrative Body

If the chief administrative body accepts the report, that body might choose one of the following:

A. The administrative body could assign all the recommendations to a qualified and interested person or persons for implementation.

B. The administrative body could assign a given function, with chosen recommendations, to an existing board. For example: The worship section might be assigned to the Board of Elders.

C. The administrative board could recommend that a new board be established. A Board of Older Adult Ministry might be initiated. This board would function like other boards and carry forward the implementation of the chosen congregational enhancements for ministry among older adults. Members could also develop new recommendations.

D. The administrative body could determine other avenues of implementation.

The administrative group will do well to authorize the study committee or a new committee to monitor the implementation process and, as desirable, propose additional ministry actions for consideration. A new committee should include members of the study committee to assure continuity.

12

The Good News about Jesus Christ: Trustworthy and Powerful to Save and Transform Lives

There is one power, and one power only, that moves and enables us and others to intentionally enhance ministry among older adults whose numbers among us continue to increase. That power is the saving power of the Gospel, the Good News about Jesus Christ. It was this power that saved St. Paul from the punishment and slavery of sin and transformed his life. About the Gospel's power to save, Paul wrote to the Christians in Rome, "I am not ashamed of the gospel, for it is the power of God for salvation to everyone who believes" (Romans 1:16). To Timothy he declared, "The saying is trustworthy and deserving of full acceptance, that Christ Jesus came into the world to save sinners, of whom I am the foremost" (1 Timothy 1:15).

About the Gospel's power to create lives anew, Paul taught the Corinthian Christians, "[I]f anyone is in Christ, he is a new creation. The old has passed away; behold, the new has come" (2 Corinthians 5:17). He testified to the Ephesians that he and all who have faith in Jesus "are His workmanship, created in Christ Jesus for good works, which God prepared beforehand, that we should walk in them" (Ephesians 2:10). As St. Paul wrote to the Philippians, "[I]t is God who works in you, both to will and to work for His good pleasure" (Philippians 2:13).

It is the Good News about Jesus Christ that moves us to love and serve others, also older adults. We love because God loves us (1 John 4:19). And it is this ability to love, generated in us by the love of God for us, which causes us to love others. St. John reveals, "By this we know love, that He laid down His life for us, and we ought to lay down our lives for the brothers. But if anyone has the world's goods and sees his brother in need, yet closes his heart against him, how does God's love abide in him? Little children, let us not love in word or talk but in deed and in truth" (1 John 3:16–18).

13 Conclusion

More and more people are retiring because increasing numbers of people are living to retirement age. In turn, more and more people live longer in retirement today either because they retire earlier than in past years and/or because they live longer than people in past generations.

A large number of contemporary retirees are members of Christ's Church, and their number is expanding by leaps and bounds. On the one hand, this large company of people provides the Church with the challenge of ministering intentionally and faithfully to older adult members. On the other hand, the increasing number of older Christians provides the Church with a growing number of Christians that are remarkably motivated and equipped by the experiences of many years to serve God and others, both fellow Christians and non-Christians, the young and the old. Older adults are God's gifts to His Church for accomplishing the mission of the Church. The present is very much a time for the Church to foster more intensive ministry among older adults, ministry to and by them as we serve with them.

Retirement years give older adults singular opportunity, as they prayerfully seek the guidance of God, to reconfigure their callings as God's people. The understanding of the Christian calling elevates the significance and possibilities of their lives to new heights. What an exciting time retirement years can be for all of us, either now or in the future!

Surrounded by the love of God, we can and will intentionally enhance ministry among older adults in God-directed and goal-driven ways. We can and will do this by the way we personally live and serve within our Christian congregations.

> In this the love of God was made manifest among us, that God sent His only Son into the world, so that we might live through Him. In this is love, not that we have loved God but that He loved us and sent His Son to be the propitiation for our sins. Beloved, if God so loved us, we also ought to love one another. No one has ever seen God; if we love one another, God abides in us and His love is perfected in us. (1 John 4:9–12)

Wonderful, indeed, is the love of God for us! His love enables us fully to express our Christian callings by serving others and by helping people to allow God to work through them for the benefit of people of the Church and world. At every age we can make our lives count for others. So it is that we do not neglect to minister among older adults. The love of Christ compels us to minister, especially to the older adults among us as their life journeys continue. May this book aid us in this ministry. The ministry of older adults, in turn, will enrich the lives of all of us no matter what our age may be.

Appendix A

Sample Forms

"Total Membership" and "Communicant Members 60 Years of Age and Older" forms and "Survey for Older Adults Ministries" are adapted from the *Older Adult Ministries Prep Book*, a study guide from the Post-Seminary Applied Learning and Support (PALS) program, created by the Commission on Ministerial Growth and Support of The Lutheran Church—Missouri Synod.

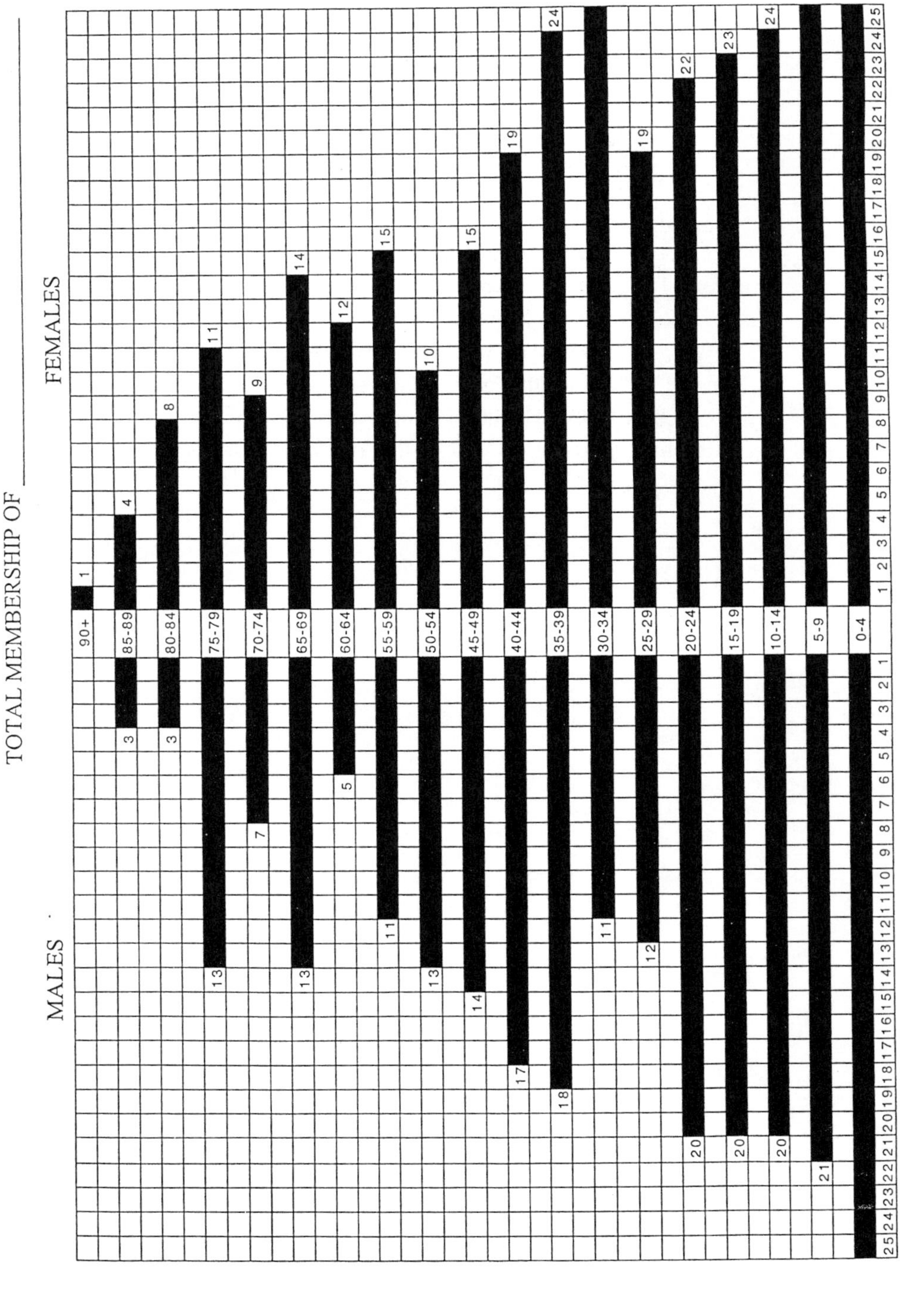
TOTAL MEMBERSHIP OF
MALES
FEMALES
90+
85-89
80-84
75-79
70-74
65-69
60-64
55-59
50-54
45-49
40-44
35-39
30-34
25-29
20-24
15-19
10-14
5-9
0-4

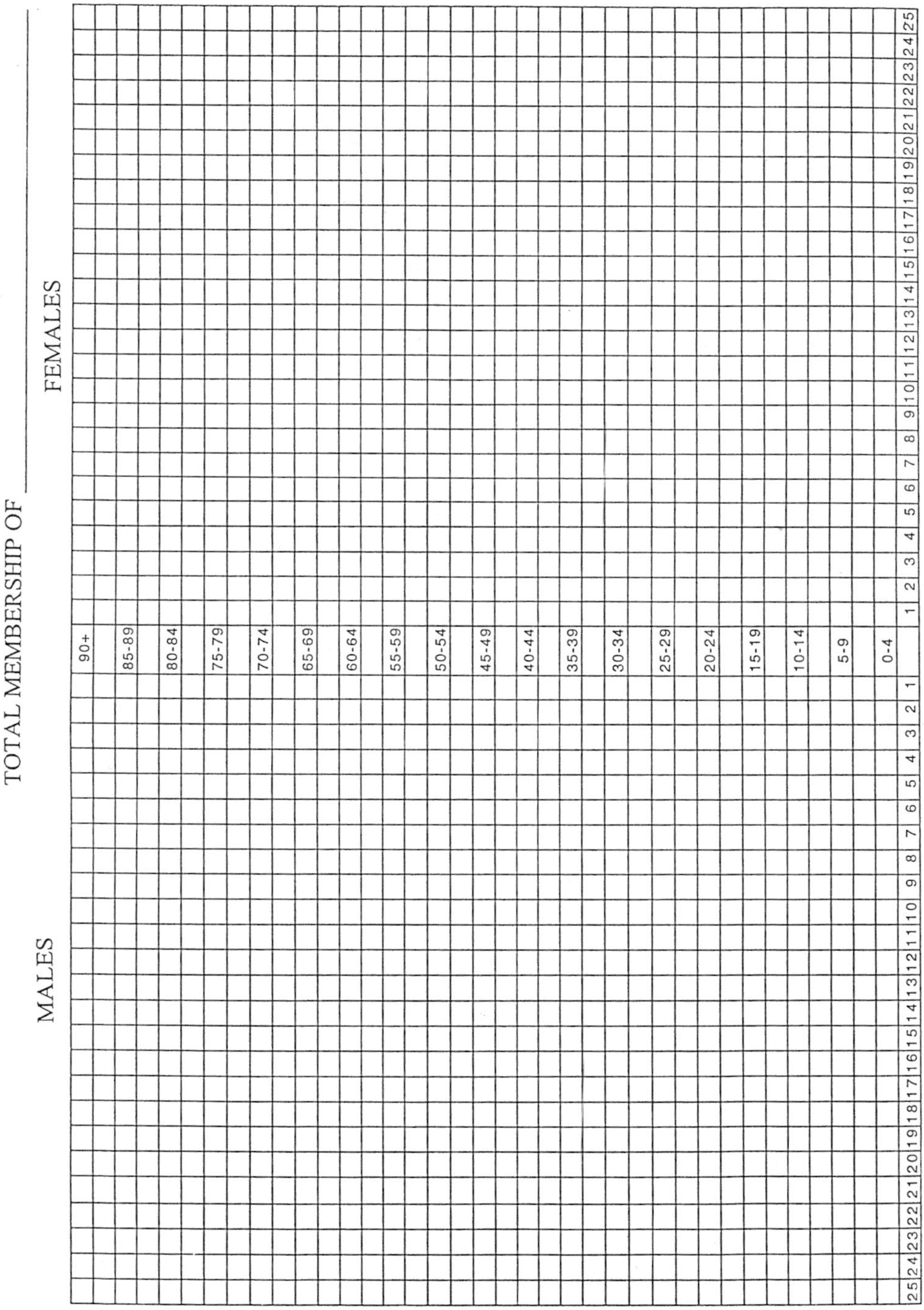
TOTAL MEMBERSHIP OF ____
MALES
FEMALES
90+
85-89
80-84
75-79
70-74
65-69
60-64
55-59
50-54
45-49
40-44
35-39
30-34
25-29
20-24
15-19
10-14
5-9
0-4
25 24 23 22 21 20 19 18 17 16 15 14 13 12 11 10 9 8 7 6 5 4 3 2 1
1 2 3 4 5 6 7 8 9 10 11 12 13 14 15 16 17 18 19 20 21 22 23 24 25

COMMUNICANT MEMBERS
60 YEARS OF AGE
AND OLDER

MEN ____________ WOMEN ____________

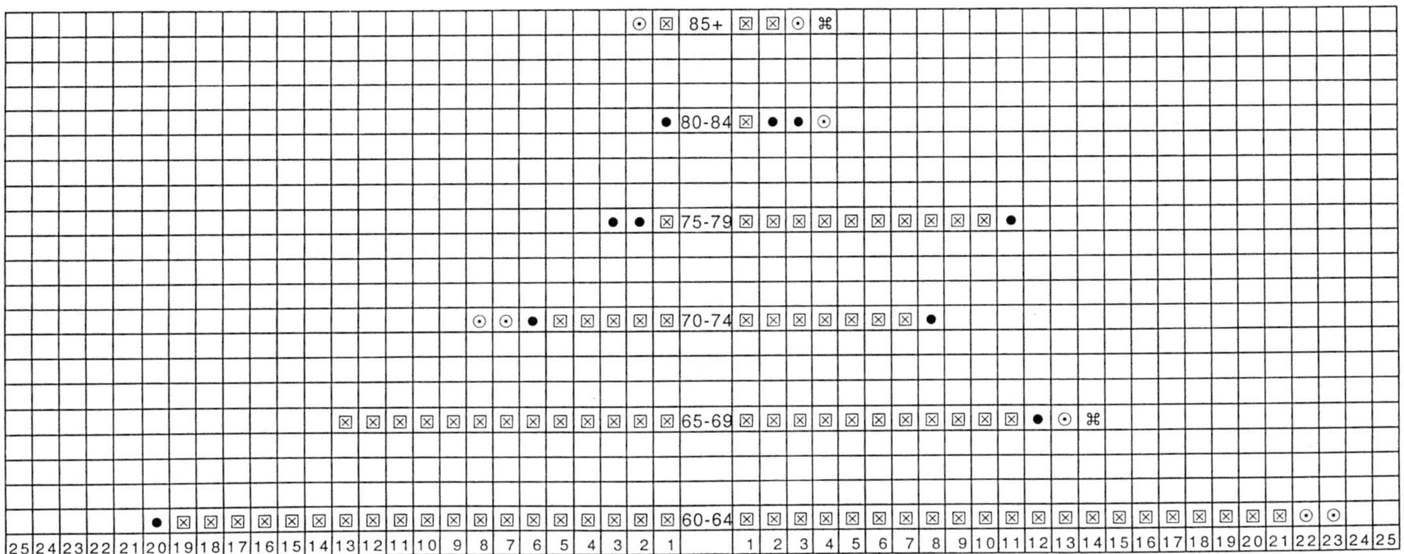

KEY

☒ The Self-Sufficient - Mobile - Up and About
⊙ The Periodic Shut-In - Sickly - Limited Social Life
♦ Residing in a Retirement Center
● The Self-Sufficient but Needs Some Assistance
■ Shut-Ins - Living Alone or w/Relatives - Spend More Time Shut-In Than Socializing
⌘ Residing In a Nursing Home

COMMUNICANT MEMBERS
60 YEARS OF AGE
AND OLDER

MEN __________ WOMEN __________

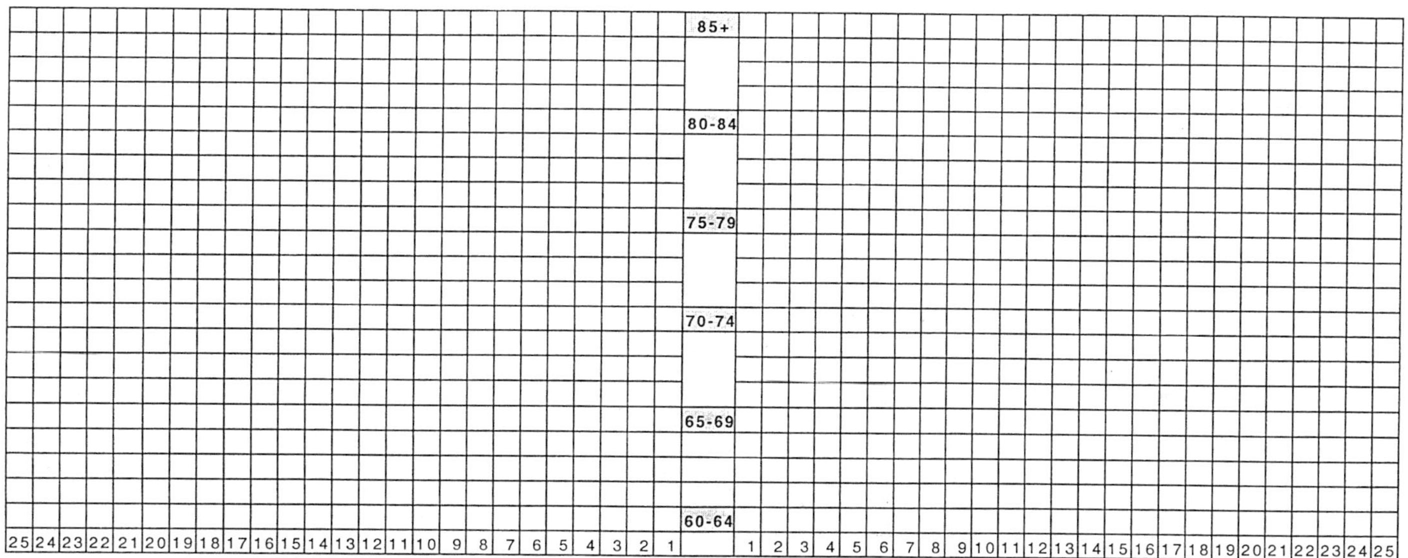

KEY

- ☒ The Self-Sufficient - Mobile - Up and About
- ⊙ The Periodic Shut-In - Sickly - Limited Social Life
- ♦ Residing in a Retirement Center
- ● The Self-Sufficient but Needs Some Assistance
- ■ Shut-Ins - Living Alone or w/Relatives - Spend More Time Shut-In Than Socializing
- ⌘ Residing In a Nursing Home

SURVEY FOR OLDER ADULTS MINISTRIES

You may determine at what age you consider persons to become older adults. For example, you might choose 55, 60, or 65 as the beginning age for this survey. Feel free to amend this form to make it more useful for your situation.

Congregation name: ______________________________

Address: ______________________________

Number of baptized members: ______________________________

Number of communing members: ______________________________

Estimated percent of older adult members: ______________________________

Size of community: ______________________________

1. Does your congregation currently have any of the following groups or activities organized primarily for older adults? (Check all that apply.)

    ____ Transportation assistance
    ____ Widow/Widower group
    ____ Housing counseling
    ____ Telephone care ministry
    ____ Home care services
    ____ Bereavement counseling
    ____ House care
    ____ Couples club
    ____ Senior group
    ____ Visitation ministry
    ____ Bible classes
    ____ Adult education
    ____ Other (specify) ______________

2. Who in your parish has the primary responsibility for older adult ministry? (Check only one.)

    ____ Pastor
    ____ Lay committee
    ____ Other professional staff
    ____ Volunteer lay member
    ____ No individual or committee has the responsibility for this ministry.
    ____ Other (explain)

3. Listed below are a number of programs or groups common to many parishes. Please check the ones in your parish that involve older adults as active participants.

    ____ Voters assembly
    ____ Elders
    ____ Stewardship
    ____ Social ministry
    ____ Altar guild
    ____ Prayer chain
    ____ Men's organization
    ____ Church council
    ____ Evangelism
    ____ Sunday School
    ____ Youth ministry
    ____ Couples club
    ____ Women's organization
    ____ Other ______________

4. Does your congregation offer any of the following special services for older adults? (Check all that apply.)
   _____ Volunteer opportunities for retirees
   _____ In-home assistance for those who are homebound
   _____ Transportation to the grocery store, physician's office, etc.
   _____ Home repair assistance
   _____ Large print materials
   _____ Information regarding community services
   _____ Informal respite care program
   _____ Barrier-free access to and in the church building as well as other facilities
   _____ Information on sessions about ethical issues

5. Describe any type of intergenerational opportunities your congregation has for older adults to work or socialize with those of other age groups.

   ____

   ____

   ____

   ____

   ____

6. As you review the questionnaire, what are some of your conclusions?

   ____

   ____

   ____

   ____

   ____

OLDER ADULTS INQUIRY FORM[1]

(The congregation is to determine the age range of older adults to be visited.)

This form is to be used by volunteer visitors who, making appointments in advance, visit older adults. Two copies are to be available, one for the visitor and one for the person being visited. During the visit the visitor is to read aloud the survey questions while the person being interviewed silently reads along. Adequate time is to be allowed for the interviewed person to answer the questions. The visitor is encouraged to aid the interviewed person by writing responses on the survey form for the person answering.

Date: ______________________________

Name: ______________________________

Address: ______________________________

Telephone: ______________________________

Interviewer's Name: ______________________________

Mark all appropriate responses.

1. Gender: ____ Female ____ Male
2. Birth Date: ______________________________
3. Status: ____ Single ____ Married ____ Widowed ____ Divorced
4. Do you live alone? ____ Yes ____ No
   If no, with whom do you live?

   ____
5. In the event of an emergency, if you need help or become ill or disabled, is there someone you could turn to for assistance?
   ____ Yes ____ No
   Name and Address of Contact Person(s):

   ____
6. During the past week,
   How many times did you have visitors? ____
   How many times did you visit someone else? ____
   How many times did you go shopping? ____
   What other places did you visit?

   ____

   ____

   How many times did you talk with a relative or friend on the telephone? ____

7. Note problems, if any, you have with the place where you live.

____
____
____
____

8. How do you rate your general health?
   ____ Excellent ____ Good ____ Fair

9. Were you ever employed outside the home? ____ Yes ____ No
   If yes, what occupation(s) did you pursue?

____
____
____
____

10. Are you able to attend worship services at church?
    ____ Yes ____ No
    How often do you attend? ____ Weekly ____ Monthly ____ Occasionally
    Other ______________________________

11. Transportation:
    a. I need transportation to: ____ church ____ work
    ____ physician's office ____ shopping ____ other
    b. I can help transport others to:
    ____

12. Home repair and maintenance service:
    a. I need assistance with: ____ yard care ____ painting ____ cooking
    ____ cleaning ____ plumbing ____ moving items ____ carpentry
    ____ changing locks ____ other
    b. I am able to help others with home repairs by:

____
____
____
____

13. Home assistance service:
    a. I need help with: ____ grocery shopping ____ cleaning ____ cooking
    ____ sewing ____ laundry ____ correspondence ____ paying bills

14. Healthcare service:
   a. I need information about: ____ medical care ____ dental care
   ____ home care
   b. I can help with healthcare by:

   ____

   ____

15. Legal and financial service:
   a. I need assistance with: ____ Social Security
   ____ will and estate planning
   ____ budget planning ____ retirement planning ____ other
   b. I can help with legal and financial planning by:

   ____

   ____

16. Personal contacts:
   a. I would like: ____ daily telephone calls ____ friendly visitors
   ____ cards and letters ____ other
   b. I can help with providing personal contacts by:

   ____

   ____

17. Spiritual care:
   a. I would like: ____ pastoral counseling ____ visits by members
   ____ Holy Communion ____ Bible study and devotional materials
   ____ other
   b. I can help with spiritual care by:

   ____

   ____

18. Educational services:
   a. I am interested in ____ large-print books ____ audio books
   ____ video films ____ computer/internet capabilities/assistance
   b. I can help with educational services by:

   ____

   ____

19. Service opportunities:
I am interested in: ____ field trips ____ group games
____ exercise classes ____ assisting with meals ____ other

20. List programs you would like the congregation to provide for older adults.

____

____

____

____

21. List services not already mentioned that you are able and willing to provide for others.

____

____

____

____

FORM FOR MINISTRY COMMENTS AND SUGGESTIONS

The Congregational Function

Congregational Worship

Current Ministry Actions	Suggested Ministry Actions

FORM FOR MINISTRY COMMENTS AND SUGGESTIONS

The Congregational Function

Worship for the Homebound

Current Ministry Actions	Suggested Ministry Actions

FORM FOR MINISTRY COMMENTS AND SUGGESTIONS

The Congregational Function

Fellowship

Current Ministry Actions	Suggested Ministry Actions

FORM FOR MINISTRY COMMENTS AND SUGGESTIONS

The Congregational Function

Stewardship

Current Ministry Actions	Suggested Ministry Actions

FORM FOR MINISTRY COMMENTS AND SUGGESTIONS

The Congregational Function

Spiritual Care for Fellow Christians

Current Ministry Actions	Suggested Ministry Actions

FORM FOR MINISTRY COMMENTS AND SUGGESTIONS

The Congregational Function

Spiritual Care for Non-Christians

Current Ministry Actions	Suggested Ministry Actions

FORM FOR MINISTRY COMMENTS AND SUGGESTIONS

The Congregational Function

Physical Care for Christians and Non-Christians
Daily Living Care

Current Ministry Actions	Suggested Ministry Actions

FORM FOR MINISTRY COMMENTS AND SUGGESTIONS

The Congregational Function

Physical Care for Christians and Non-Christians
Health Care

Current Ministry Actions	Suggested Ministry Actions

Appendix B

Resources

The resources that follow are cited by various writers as helpful in providing ministry among older adults. Like all resources used in Christian ministry, they must be viewed and used in the light of Biblical teachings, especially the life-saving Gospel of Jesus Christ.

Books

Arn, Win, and Charles Arn. *Catch the Age Wave: A Handbook for Effective Ministry with Senior Adults.* Kansas City, Mo.: Beacon Hill Press of Kansas City, 1999.

Bergstrom, Leona, and Richard Bergstrom. *Amazing Grays.* Church Health: Bellingham, Wash., 2000.

Bosak, Susan V., and Laurie McGaw. *Something to Remember Me By.* Ontario, Canada: The Communication Project, 1997.

———. *Building Connections Between Young and Old.* Ontario, Canada: The Communication Project, n.d.

Boyd, Malcolm. *Simple Grace: A Mentor's Guide to Growing Older.* Louisville, Ky.: Westminster John Knox Press, 2001.

Buford, Bob. *Stuck in Halftime: Reinvesting Your One and Only Life.* Grand Rapids: Zondervan, 2001.

Carl, William J. Jr., ed. *Graying Gracefully: Preaching to Older Adults.* Louisville Ky.: Westminster John Knox Press, 1997.

Carlson, Dosia. *Engaging in Ministry with Older Adults.* Washington DC: Alban Institute, 1997.

Carter, Jimmy. *The Virtues of Aging.* New York: Ballantine Publishing Group, 1998.

Dychtwald, Ken. *Age Power: How the 21st Century Will Be Ruled by the New Old*. New York: Jeremy P. Tarcher/Putnam, 1999.

———, and Joe Flower. *Age Wave: The Challenges and Opportunities of an Aging America*. Los Angeles: Jeremy P. Tarcher, Inc., 1989.

Fischer, Kathleen. *Winter Grace*. Nashville: Upper Room Books, 1998.

Freedman, Marc. *Prime Time: How Baby Boomers Will Revolutionize Retirement and Transform America*. New York: Public Affairs, 1999.

Fry, Patricia L. *Creative Grandparenting: Across the Miles*. Liguori, Mo.: Liguori, 1997.

Fowler, Ruth. *As We Grow Old*. Valley Forge, Pa.: Judson Press, 1998.

Gallagher, David P. *Senior Adult Ministry in the 21st Century: Step-by-Step Strategies for Reaching People Over 50*. Loveland, Colo.: Group, 2002.

Garmatz, Robert W. *Never Too Old: How to Involve Older Adults in Your Church*. St. Louis: Concordia, 1992.

Gentzler, Richard H. Jr. *Designing an Older Adult Ministry*. Nashville: Discipleship Resources, 1999.

———, and Donald F. Clingan. *Aging: God's Challenge to Church and Synagogue*. Nashville: Discipleship Resources, 1996.

Godwin, Johnnie C. *Life's Best Chapter—Retirement*. Birmingham: New Hope Publishers, 2000.

Harvey, L. James, and Jackie Harvey. *Every Day is Saturday: A Christian Guide to a Fantastic Retirement*. St. Louis: Concordia, 2000.

Hawkins, Melissa O. *Preparing Participants for Intergenerational Interaction*. Binghamton, N.Y.: Haworth Press, 1999.

Hayman, Sandra W. *My Turn: Caring For Aging Parents and Other Elderly Loved Ones*. Tallahassee, Fla.: Magnolia Publications, 1996.

Hollies, Linda, and Giraurd C. Hollies. *Pilgrim Prayers for Grandmothers Raising Grandchildren*. Cleveland: Pilgrim Press, 2002.

Johnson, Richard P. *Creating a Successful Retirement: Finding Peace and Purpose*. Liguori, MO: Liguori Lifespan, 1999.

———. *The 12 Keys to Spiritual Vitality—Powerful Lessons on Living Agelessly*. Liguori, Mo.: Liguori, 1998.

Knapp, James L. *The Graying of the Flock: A New Model for Ministry*. Siloam Springs, Ark.: Leafwood Publishers, 2003.

Knippel, Charles T. *When Addictions Threaten*. St. Louis: Concordia, 2000.

Knutson, Lois. *Understanding the Senior Adult*. Bethesda, Md.: Alban Institute, 1999.

Koenig, Harold G., with Tracy Lamar and Betty Lamar. *A Gospel for the Mature Years: Finding Fulfillment by Knowing and Using Your Gifts*. Binghamton, N.Y.: Haworth Pastoral Press, 1997.

Koenig, Harold G., and Andrew J. Weaver. *Counseling Troubled Older Adults: A Handbook for Pastors and Religious Caregivers*. Nashville: Abingdon Press, 1997.

McCall, Junietta Baker. *Grief Education for Caregivers of the Elderly*. Binghamton, N.Y.: Haworth Pastoral Press, 1999.

McIntosh, Gary L. *One Church, Four Generations: Understanding and Reaching All Ages in Your Church*. Grand Rapids: Baker Books, 2002.

McKim, Donald K., ed. *God Never Forgets: Faith, Hope, and Alzheimer's Disease*. Louisville, Ky.: Westminster John Knox Press, 1997.

Mann, Leonard. *Treasures Found in Passing*. Harrisburg, Pa.: Morehouse Publishing, 2001.

Miller, James E. *Autumn Wisdom*. Minneapolis: Augsburg, 1995.

———. *The Caregivers Book*. Minneapolis: Augsburg, 1996.

Saussy, Carroll. *The Art of Growing Old*. Minneapolis: Augsburg, 1998.

Savishinsky, Joel S. *Breaking the Watch: The Meanings of Retirement in America*. Ithaca, N.Y.: Cornell University Press, 2000.

Simmons, Henry C., and Jane Wilson. *Soulful Aging*. Macon, Ga.: Smyth and Helwys, 2001.

———, and E. Graig MacBean. *Thriving After 55*. Richmond, Va.: Prime Press, 2000.

———, and Mark A. Peters. *With God's Oldest Friends: Pastoral Visiting in the Nursing Home*. New York: Paulist Press, 1996.

Sonnenberg, Roger. *Celebrating Life as Grandparents*. St. Louis: Concordia, 1993.

Sullender R. Scott. *Losses in Late Life: A New Way of Walking with God*. New York: Paulist Press, 1989.

Tanneberg, Ward, and Stephen Taylor. *Seasons for the Spirit*. Colorado Springs, Colo.: Lion Publishing, 1998.

Vaillant, George E. *Aging Well*. Boston: Little, Brown, and Company, 2002.

Wicks, Robert J. *After Fifty*. New York: Paulist Press, 1997.

Wiggin, Eric. *The Gift of Grandparenting*. Wheaton, Ill.: Tyndale, 2001.

Devotional Materials

Bayer, Les, ed. *Devotions for the Chronologically Gifted.* St. Louis: Concordia, 1999.

Dunson, Miriam. *A Very Present Help: Psalms Studies for Older Adults.* Louisville, Ky.: Geneva Press, 1999.

Kuntz, Arnold G. *Joy in the Journey.* St. Louis: Concordia, 1992.

Morgan, Richard L. *No Wrinkles on the Soul.* Nashville: Upper Room Books, 1990.

Paustian, Henry E. *Listen! God is Speaking to You! God's Word for Seniors.* Milwaukee: Northwestern, 1994.

Rabior, William. *Prayers for Later Years.* Liguori, Mo.: Liguori Press, 2001.

Rainwater, Pearl. *Grandma Speaks.* Milwaukee: Northwestern, 1994.

———. *Grandma's Voice.* Milwaukee: Northwestern, 1998.

Magazines and Journals

Innovations: The Journal of the National Council on the Aging. The National Council on the Aging, 300 D Street, SW, #801, Washington DC 20024. www.ncoa.org.

Mature Living. LifeWay Christian Resources of the Southern Baptist Convention, One LifeWay Plaza, Nashville, TN 37234. www.lifeway.com.

Newsletters and Bulletins

"AARP (American Association of Retired Persons) Bulletin." 601 E. Street NW, Washington DC 20049. 888-687-2277. www.aarp.org.

"Center Sage." Center on Aging and Older Adult Ministries, General Board of Discipleship of The United Methodist Church, P.O. Box 340003, Nashville, TN 37203. 877-899-2780. www.aging-umc.org.

"Engaging the Aging. " Lutheran Senior Services, 709 South Laclede Station Road, St. Louis, MO 63119-4911. 877-363-1211. www.lssmo.org

"The Journal of Intergenerational Relationships." 121 University Place #407, Pittsburgh, PA 15260. 412-648-7155. http://jir.ucsur.pitt.edu

Videos

Aging Parents. Liguori Publications, One Liguori Drive, Liguori, MO 63057. 800-325-9521.

A Late Frost. Contains 10 segments, five minutes each, dealing with issues of growing old. Seraphim Communications, Inc., 1568 Eustis St., St. Paul, MN 55108. 800-733-3413.

At Death's Door: Facing the Terminal Illness of a Loved One. Paraclete Video Production, Paraclete Press, Inc., P.O. Box 1568, Orleans, MA 02653. 800-451-5006.

Beyond the News: Facing Death. Three families tell their stories of facing issues surrounding death and dying. Mennonite Media, 1251 Virginia Ave., Harrisonburg, VA 22802. 800-999-3534.

Elders and Families. Help for families in planning quality care with their dependent elders. Northwest Media, Inc., 326 West 12th Ave., Eugene, OR 97401. 800-777-6636.

Facing Death. A series of two tapes for caregivers (volunteer and professional) of the terminally ill and their family and friends. Family Experiences Productions, Inc., P.O. Box 5879, Austin, TX 78763. 512-494-0338.

Facing My Own Suffering and Loss. St. Anthony Messenger Press, 28 W. Liberty St., Cincinnati, OH 45202. 800-488-0488.

Home Sweet Home: How to Help Older Adults Live Independently. (Available to Thrivent Members.) Thrivent Financial for Lutherans, 4321 N. Ballard Road, Appleton, WI 54919. 800-847-4836.

I Grow Old. Elder abuse through the eyes of those who have lived through it. Terra Nova Films. Gerontology Library Audiovisual Collection, University of Southern California University Park, MC0191, Los Angeles, CA 90089.

Wrestling with Angels. Part 2: "Why Me?" Author Philip Yancy seeks to help people find hope in the face of suffering. Trinity Church, 74 Trinity Place, New York, NY 10006. 212-602-0800.

Organizations and Agencies

American Association of Retired Persons
601 E. Street NW
Washington DC 20049
888-687-2277
www.aarp.org

Association of Lutheran Older Adults (ALOA)
The Lutheran Center—1st Floor
700 Light Street
Baltimore, MD 21230
800-930-ALOA
www.aloaserves.org

Center for Aging, Religion and Spirituality
Luther Seminary
2481 Como Ave.
St. Paul, MN 55108-1496
651-641-3581
http://www.aging-religion-spirituality.com/

Eldercare Locator
800-677-1116
www.eldercare.gov

Elderhostel
11 Avenue de Lafayette
Boston, MA 02111-1746
877-426-8056
www.elderhostel.org

ElderWeb
1305 Chadwick Drive
Normal, IL 61761
www.elderweb.com

The Lutheran Church—Missouri Synod World Relief and Human Care
1333 S. Kirkwood Rd.
St. Louis, MO 63122
800-248-1930, Ext. 1380
www.lcms.org

Luther Hostel
Lutheran Outdoor Ministries of Florida
3815 West State Street
Tampa, Florida 33609
813-801-9600
http://www.lomfla.org/

National Council on the Aging
300 D Street, SW
Suite 801
Washington DC 20024
202-479-1200
www.ncoa.org

National Hospice and Palliative Care Organization (NHPCO)
1700 Diagonal Road, Suite 625
Alexandria, VA 22314
703-837-1500
www.nhpco.org

Thrivent Financial for Lutherans
4321 N. Ballard Rd.
Appleton, WI 54919
800-847-4836
www.thrivent.org

(Review the sidebar topics that have to do with ministry to older adults at http://thrivent.com/planning/index.html. Look especially at: Elder Care, Life Events, Retirement Planning, Retirement Strategies and Products, and Estate Strategies.)

Additional Internet Resources

Administration on Aging
www.aoa.gov

The AgeNet Eldercare Network
www.agenet.com

Alzheimer's Association
www.alz.org

American Association of Retired Persons
www.aarp.org

Association for Lifelong Adult Ministry
www.senioradultministry.com

Association of Lutheran Older Adults
www.aloaserves.org

The Christian Association of Senior Adult Ministries
www.gocasa.org

Center for Aging, Religion and Spirituality
www.aging-religion-spirituality.com

Eldercare Locator
www.eldercare.gov

Elderhostel
www.elderhostel.org

Federal Interagency Forum on Aging-Related Statistics
www.agingstats.gov

GRANDtimes.com
www.grandtimes.com

Habitat for Humanity
www.habitat.org

Health and Age
www.healthandage.com

Health Finder
www.healthfinder.gov

iGrandparents.com
www.igrandparents.com

Laborers for Christ (The Lutheran Church—Missouri Synod)
http://old.mission.lcms.org/laborers

Legacy Project
www.tcpnow.com

Methodist Center on Aging and Older Adult Ministries
www.aging-umc.org

The National Council on the Aging
(also see National Interfaith Coalition on Aging)
www.ncoa.org

National Hospice and Palliative Care Organization
www.nhpco.org

National Institute on Aging
www.nia.nih.gov

Oasis—Enriching the Lives of Mature Adults
www.oasisnet.org

Resources from A–Z for Senior Adults
www.refdesk.com/seniors.html

SeniorNet
www.seniornet.org

Significant Living
www.christianprimetimers.org

Social Security Online
www.ssa.gov

Temple University Center for Intergenerational Learning
www.temple.edu/cil

United States Department of Health and Human Services
www.hhs.gov

United States Treasury (Internal Revenue Service Information)
www.ustreas.gov

WidowNet
www.widownet.org

Other Local Resources to Consult

- AARP local chapter
- Area Agency on Aging
- Continuing education courses at local educational facilities
- Directories (local)
- Hospitals
- Lutheran agencies
- LCMS district office
- Social Security Administration

- State Older Adult Office
- University extension courses
- United Way
- Visiting Nurses Association

Notes

Chapter 1

1. U.S. Census Bureau, http://www.census.gov/main/www/cen2000.html.
2. Lisa Hetzel and Annetta Smith, "The 65 Years and Over Population: 2000," Census 2000 Brief, www.census.gov/prod/2001pubs/c2kbr01-10.pdf.
3. University of Wisconsin System Administration Office of Staff Benefits and Payroll Policy, Employee Benefits, "Are You Considering Early Retirement?" University of Wisconsin System, http://www.uwsa.edu/hr/benefits/retsav/early.htm; United and Food Commercial Workers, Unions and Employees, "Retirement Ages and Types," www.ufcwmidwest.org/pension/pen_ages.html#early; William J. Wiatrowski, "Changing Retirement Age: Ups and Downs," *Monthly Labor Review* (April 2001): 1.
4. National Academy Of Social Insurance, "Fact Sheet: Social Security Retirement Age at a Glance," http://www.nasi.org/publications2763/publications_show.htm?doc_id=56912&name=Social%20Security.
5. Hetzel and Smith, "The 65 Years and Over Population: 2000."
6. Hetzel and Smith, "The 65 Years and Over Population: 2000."
7. Hetzel and Smith, "The 65 Years and Over Population: 2000."
8. Department of Health and Human Services, Administration on Aging, "A Profile of Older Americans: 2000," http://www.aoa.gov/prof/Statistics/profile/1_pf.asp.
9. James L. Knapp, *The Graying of the Flock: A New Model for Ministry* (Siloam Springs, Ark.: Leafwood Publishers, 2003), 11; Hetzel and Smith, "The 65 Years and Over Population: 2000."
10. Federal Interagency Forum on Aging-Related Statistics, "Older Ameri-

cans 2000: Key Indicators of Well-Being, Updated Detailed Tables," www.agingstats.gov/tables%202001/tables-healthstatus.html.

11. Department of Health and Human Services, "A Profile of Older Americans: 2000."
12. Hetzel and Smith, "The 65 Years and Over Population: 2000."
13. Department of Health and Human Services, "A Profile of Older Americans: 2000."
14. Federal Interagency Forum on Aging-Related Statistics, "Older Americans 2000: Key Indicators of Well-Being, Updated Detailed Tables."
15. "Older Adults are 'New Blessing' to Church," *Taking Steps*, a publication of the Older Adults Ministries of the Human Care Ministries of The Lutheran Church—Missouri Synod (September 1999): 1.
16. Administration on Aging, "A Profile of Older Americans: 2000."
17. Administration on Aging, "A Profile of Older Americans: 2000."
18. Administration on Aging, "A Profile of Older Americans: 2000."
19. Administration on Aging, "A Profile of Older Americans: 2000."
20. Administration on Aging, "A Profile of Older Americans: 2000."
21. Administration on Aging, "A Profile of Older Americans: 2000."

Chapter 2

1. AC IV, 1–3 (Tappert, 30).
2. Small Catechism, "The Second Article: Redemption," 4 (Tappert, 345).
3. LW 49:268–69; also see full text of letter on 267–71.

Chapter 3

1. "Helping Older Adults Continue Their Spiritual Journey," *Taking Steps*, a publication of the Older Adults Ministries of the Human Care Ministries of The Lutheran Church—Missouri Synod (September 1999): 4.
2. Federal Interagency Forum on Aging-Related Statistics, "Detailed Tables, Health Status—Indicator 12: Life Expectancy," www.agingstats.gov/tables%202001/tables-healthstatus.html.
3. Administration on Aging, "Older Population by Age: 1900–2050," www.aoa.gov/prof/Statistics/online_stat_data/AgePop2050.asp.
4. University of Wisconsin System Administration Office of Staff Benefits and Payroll Policy, Employee Benefits, "Are You Considering Early Retirement ?"; United and Food Commercial Workers, Unions and Employees, "Retirement Ages and Types"; Wiatrowski, "Changing Retirement Age: Ups and Downs," 1.

5. Todd Wilken, "The Six Commandments of the Boomers," *The New Issues, Etc., Journal* 1, no. 2, www.issuesetc.org/resource/journals/v1n2wlkn.htm.
6. LW 24:69–70.
7. Small Catechism, "The Third Article: Sanctification," 6 (Tappert, 345).
8. Large Catechism, "The Third Article," 38 (Tappert, 415).
9. LW 3:128.
10. LW 8:75.
11. LW 3:118.
12. LW 4:288.
13. LW 3:130.
14. LW 3:130.
15. LW 3:130.
16. LW 43:226.
17. LW 46:250.
18. From *God at Work: Your Christian Vocation in All of Life* by Gene Veith, copyright 2002, 162. Used by permission of Crossway Books, a ministry of Good News Publishers, Wheaton, Illinois 60187, www.gnpcb.org.
19. LW 3:290, *my emphasis.*
20. LW 24:221.
21. Win Arn and Charles Arn, *Catch the Age Wave: A Handbook for Effective Ministry with Senior Adults* (Kansas City, Mo.: Beacon Hill Press of Kansas City, 1999), 13.
22. Arn and Arn, *Catch the Age Wave*, 29, 31.
23. Arn and Arn, *Catch the Age Wave*, 27–28.

Chapter 4

1. Small Catechism, "The Third Article: Sanctification," 6 (Tappert, 345).
2. Gary L. McIntosh, *One Church, Four Generations: Understanding and Reaching All Ages in Your Church* (Grand Rapids: Baker Books, 2002), 17.
3. McIntosh, *One Church, Four Generations*, 232.

Chapter 5

1. AC VII, 1–2 (Tappert, 32).

2. AC VIII, 1 (Tappert, 33).

Chapter 8

1. Small Catechism, "The First Article: Creation," 2 (Tappert, 345).

Chapter 9

1. James L. Knapp, *The Graying of the Flock* (Siloam Springs, Ark.: Leafwood Publishers, 2003), 11.
2. Knapp, *Graying of the Flock*, 11.
3. David P. Gallagher, *Senior Adult Ministry in the 21st Century* (Loveland, Colo.: Group, 2002), 6.

Chapter 10

1. RetirementOptions.com, "Your Retirement Options," www.retirementoptions.com/pages/options.asp.
2. AARP, "Baby Boomers Envision Retirement II—Key Findings," Prepared for AARP by RoperASW, http://assets.aarp.org/rgcenter/econ/boomers_envision_1.pdf.
3. AARP, "Baby Boomers Envision Retirement II—Key Findings."
4. Kerby Anderson, "Disillusionment in the 1990s," Probe Ministries, www.leaderu.com/orgs/probe/docs/disillus.html.
5. Senior Journal.com, "Zoomer Day Survey Predicts End to Aging Stigma; Zoomers Foresee a Retirement That is 'Born to be Wild,'" www.seniorjournal.com/NEWS/Features/03-23-01Zoomers.htm; Dena Amoruso, "Boomers Change Retirement Expectations," RealtyTimes, http://realtytimes.com/printrtpages/20010202_boomers.htm.
6. Amoruso, "Boomers Change Retirement Expectations."
7. Amoruso, "Boomers Change Retirement Expectations."
8. Allen Unrau, "Will Boomers Bust the Fear of Aging?" *Retirement with a Purpose*, www.retirementwithapurpose.com/aubustaging.html.
9. Gary L. McIntosh, *Generation Tips*, "They're Not Babies Anymore," www.wesleyan.org/ssd/generationtips/generation.htm
10. Bruce Edwards, "Boomers and Ministry," *CASA Energizing Seniors* (Summer 2003): 1–2.
11. *The Lutheran Hymnal* (St. Louis: Concordia, 1941), no. 478, vv.1–2.
12. *Lutheran Worship* (St. Louis: Concordia, 1982), 148.
13. National Institute of Mental Health, "Older Adults: Depression and Suicide Facts," www.nimh.nih.gov/publicat/elderlydepsuicide.cfm.

14. National Institute of Mental Health, "Older Adults: Depression and Suicide Facts."
15. HealthyPlace.com Depression Community, "Depression in Elderly," www.healthyplace.com/communities/depression/elderly.asp.
16. *University of Cincinnati E-Briefs*, October 1999, www.uc.edu/news/ebriefs/drugs.htm.
17. Alexandra Marks, "Illicit Drug Use Grows Among the Elderly," *The Christian Science Monitor*, www.csmonitor.com/2002/0327/p03s01-ussc.htm.
18. Alzheimer's Foundation of America, "About Alzheimer's," http://www.alzfdn.org/alzheimers/symptoms.shtml.
19. U.S. Census Bureau, "Unmarried and Single Americans Week," http://www.census.gov/Press-Release/www/2004/cb04-ffse11.pdf.
20. "Older Americans 'Shacking Up' More," http://www.cbsnews.com/stories/2002/02/30/national/printable51681d4.shtml
21. Richard Balkus and Susan Wilschke, "Treatment of Married Couples in the SSI Program," U.S. Social Security Administration, http://www.ssa.gov/policy/docs/issuepapers/ip2003-01.html.

Appendix A

1. Adapted by permission from Richard H. Gentzler Jr., *Designing an Older Adult Ministry* (Nashville: Discipleship Resources, 1999), 69–72.